Love Triangles

Discovering Jesus the Jew
in
Today's Israel

Bobbie Ann Cole

Love Triangles
Discovering Jesus the Jew in Today's Israel
Copyright © 2015 by Bobbie Ann Cole

Bobbie Ann Cole asserts the moral right to be identified as the author of this work.

Published by Scrollchest.com, NB, Canada

All rights reserved. No part of this book may be reproduced, stored in a retrieval system, or transmitted in any form or by any means, electronic or mechanical, including photocopying, reprinting and recording, except for brief quotations in printed reviews, without prior written permission of Bobbie Ann Cole (bobbie@testimonytrain.com).

Scriptures taken from the Holy Bible, New International Version®, NIV®, Copyright © 1973, 1978, 1984, 2011 by Biblica, Inc.™ Used by permission of Zondervan. All rights reserved worldwide. www.Zondervan.com The "NIV" and "New International Version" are trademarks registered in the United States, Patent and Trademark Office by Biblica, Inc.™

Print ISBN: 978-0-9917604-4-2
E-book ISBN: 978-0-9917604-5-9

Disclaimer
Every reasonable effort has been made to ensure that the information contained in this book is accurate. However, no guarantee is made regarding its accuracy or completeness. The reader assumes responsibility and liability for all actions in relation to using the provided information.

Author's Note
To avoid possible offence or embarrassment, the names of some of the persons whose stories or opinions are given in this book have been changed.

Cover design: Sandy Armstrong,
ChristianEditingServices.com

Formatting: RikHall,
WildSeasFormatting.com

Am Yisrael Chai

Psalm 133

A song of ascents. Of David.

"How good and pleasant it is when God's people live together in unity!
It is like precious oil poured on the head, running down on the beard, running down on Aaron's beard, down on the collar of his robe.
It is as if the dew of Hermon were falling on Mount Zion. For there the Lord bestows his blessing, even life forevermore."

Praise for Love Triangles

"A compellingly-written personal story of a journey to faith in Christ and beyond."
—*David Edwards - Bishop of Fredericton*

"*Love Triangles* illuminates the unexpected journey of one women's quest to come to grips with the overwhelming scope of Israel's history and legacy, contrasted by today's stark and sometimes harsh realities. This is all seen through the real life experiences of one person but don't be surprised if you find yourself on many of its pages. This book is an 'eyes wide open' must-read."
—*George Woodward, founder Israel's Peace Ministries*

"Moving and well written, Bobbie Ann Cole's story of making Aliyah to Israel with her husband, Butch, combines history, Scripture with accounts of Messianic Jews and Christians living there from around the world. With open, heartfelt honesty, Cole shares vital insights on the courage and determination that Messianic believers require to sustain their calling in Israel."
—*Ben Volman, Toronto Director, Chosen People Ministries Canada and founding Messianic Rabbi of Kehillat Eytz Chaim / Tree of Life Messianic Congregation, Toronto*

"Her love of the Land of Israel and the Scriptures shine out as the author narrates her Aliyah journey."
—*Judith Galblum Pex, author of Walk the Land, A People Tall and Smooth, Come, Stay, Celebrate*

"If you love Israel and Messiah Yeshua then you'll love *Love Triangles, Discovering Jesus the Jew in Today's Israel*. I recommend this great book to all!
—*Rev. Walter Slaughter, founder of Israel for Life*

"You feel as if you're walking the paths Jesus walked two millennia ago. Bobbie Ann Cole may have led a 'secret life,' but each page gives us an insider's look at some of her very personal experiences. If you've ever felt like a misfit, you'll be able to identify with Cole as a Messianic Jew in the 21st century."
—*Betsy Balega, author Being Mystic in Touch with God and Hosts and broadcaster Tuning in with Betsy*

"Bobbie writes in a very easy-to-read fashion which captures the depth of her personal experience and faith journey. Her book helps the reader to understand more about modern day Israel and the plight of the Messianic Jewish people. I would recommend this book to anyone seeking a greater understanding of our Jewish roots as they pertain to our Faith."
—*Vivian Osborne, Pastor's wife*

"A really enjoyable read that opened my eyes to the importance of Israel in God's plans, and the challenges facing Messianic Jews. In this book the author connects the life of Jesus to events and festivals in the Old

Testament. Her testimonies provide an excellent insight into the persecution experienced not only by today's Jews who believe in Jesus, but also by his early Jewish disciples".
> —*Trevor Fotheringham, Treasurer, Parish of Lakewood, NB, Canada*

"*Love Triangles* has a mix of personal accounts and history to inform the reader of the modern day struggles in Israel. The Nation of Israel has had a long journey and identity crisis in the search of their Messiah. Bobbie Ann Cole has done a great job bringing this timely topic to light."
> —*Brad Saunders, Sabbath Keepers Fellowship, Maine*

"*Love Triangles* is a vibrant, captivating read that effectively interweaves Israel's ancient and modern history with biblical references and the author's own personal experiences. Sparkling with intelligence and peppered with sage observations, *Love Triangles* is a spectacular labor of love born out of Cole's deep passion for both the Messiah and the country of Israel. Fearless and thought-provoking, it is a must read for anyone seeking to discover and/or better understand the impact of Jesus Christ within the context of today's rapidly evolving times."
> —*Sally Meadows, two time national award nominated singer/songwriter and author of Beneath That Star*

"One of the things I love about Israel is the way ancient and modern history collide with our present-day history in a wonderful expression of God's plan for His people. Here in Bobbie's book are a number of stories woven together from the Bible, from history and from Bobbie's own life in a perfect demonstration of how Jesus, the Jewish Messiah, reaches through history to touch both ancient and modern people, as well as Bobbie, her husband, Butch, and those they met along the way. As someone who has had the joy of visiting Israel, Bobbie's reflections took me right back to my own encounter with the Land and back to being among believers of all nations at Beit Immanuel, where I have stayed as a member of the CMJ Team. This meeting of like-minded people touched by the Spirit of God must be a foretaste of heaven."

> —Steph Cottam, Youth Worker for Church's Ministry among Jewish people (CMJ), author of Ready or Not – He is Coming

"Bobbie Ann Cole is a gifted and insightful writer. *Love Triangles* showcases her ability to provide unique perspective and to present it in an engaging and compelling work."

> —Karl Ingersoll, Chaplain Coordinator, RCMP, "J" Division, NB, Canada

"This book truly enlightens the heart to the understanding of the meaning of Aliyah within the Jewish soul."

> —Yedidia Flaquer, the Art Garage

"Bobbie has captured what matters. This book is not about theological principals; it's about love."

> —Adrian Glasspole, Secretary, British Messianic Jewish Alliance

"Bobbie Cole has opened a window onto the faith and experience of those Jewish believers who have embraced Jesus as their Messiah. With candor and an intimate knowledge of the land and its people, she weaves a

picture, together with the depth of personal experience. All believers, both Gentile and Jewish, would be well advised to read this book as its insights will add depth and understanding to Israel and to the Faith we have all inherited from the heart of Abraham. I really enjoyed reading this book, one of the best I've ever read and of great value to anyone."
—*Rev. Canon Keith Osborne, Canada*

Acknowledgements

I am grateful to all my contributors, in particular to Joshua Pex for his insights into the Israeli legal system and to "Tom" (you know who you are) for bringing theological dimensions to this book that might otherwise have passed me by.

I want to thank Stephanie Nickel for her superlative editing and critiquing of my manuscript; also Debra Englander for her critiques and Martha Bullen for her marketing-based advice.

Pastor Chuck Cohen of Intercessors for Israel Ministry has kindly allowed me to reproduce some of his prayers for Aliyah.

My dear friend Valerie Letley in England has given me wise input, as always, and Keith Osborne in Canada has encouraged and supported me. I am thankful for them both.

Above all, I want to acknowledge dear Butch, my husband who did not shy away from traveling to Israel with me, who fell in love with the Land and who has been more than willing to revive our experiences living there during the birthing of this book.

Preface

"In visions of God he took me to the land of Israel and set me on a very high mountain... He took me there, and I saw a man whose appearance was like bronze...The Man said to me, 'Son of man, look carefully and listen closely and pay attention to everything I am going to show you, for that is why you have been brought here. Tell the people of Israel everything you see'" (Ezekiel 40:2-4).

Barely a year after we married, Butch and I left Canada for Israel. No voice from heaven had thundered at us to go there. No prophetic word was spoken. We had no sense of being led to the Land.

The fact of the matter was that we had decided to move to England and the timing seemed right to leave Canada, where we had been living since our marriage. Butch's daughter and her husband were eager to take over his business looking after special care residents. However, my house in England was still rented out, until the following spring. We decided to look for a volunteer position that would bridge that six-month gap.

A guest house in Jaffa of the Church's Ministry Among Jewish People immediately came to mind. I knew something about the place since I had applied to volunteer there before. It hadn't been a fit then, but this time things worked out. Butch was excited to go to Israel for the first time and I was very happy to be going there with him.

We never intended to immigrate. The idea of exploring whether we could came during one of our evening wanderings along the esplanade from Jaffa to Tel Aviv. On our left, waves curled onto the sand; on our right, the city lights were going on like stars. All around us was vibrant life, strollers and joggers and rollerbladers weaving past.

"I want to live here!" Butch, the Canadian country boy, declared. Back home our friends and family were elbow-deep in snow.

And so, a little apprehensively, I checked out whether I could facilitate that. What bothered me more than the many wars and terrorism the young State of Israel had known since its founding was that for all its Western facade, this country was still profoundly Middle Eastern.

What I loved, but as someone relatively young in faith had never known before, was following Jesus all around the Land. That was a powerful incentive.

In our three months there, we had met Him in the Negev Desert, in Jerusalem's Old City, and on the shores of the Sea of Galilee. We had felt His presence at the volunteers' daily morning worship, when Polish, Russian, French, Dutch, Korean, Canadian and English volunteers sang hymns together and prayed in our own languages. We had

LOVE TRIANGLES

discovered that even though the country was constantly on high military alert, there was what Butch referred to as "that safe, spiritual feeling," a serenity rooted in faith, a trust that God "has it."

Butch felt what I had felt every time I came to Israel. This little country, hardly bigger than New Jersey, the USA's fifth smallest state, about the size of the country of Wales, is diverse and inspirational, uplifting and stunningly beautiful. All of history is here: ancient, recent, and unfolding daily. On the international stage today, Israel is the loudest little nation in the world.

The climate is as varied as the landscape. "You can be in Jerusalem and it's snowing," Butch would say, "and drive for forty-five minutes and be in your bathing suit." The distance between the two is a mere forty miles, sixty-seven kilometers. During the winter, I would fill a heavy bag with coat, hat, and gloves for a day out, only to strip down to a t-shirt upon my return to the Mediterranean coast where we lived.

Israel is a nation of complex, brave, and resilient survivors. Native-born Israelis are called *sabras.* Sabra is a prickly pear, the tall cactus that lines crop fields all over Israel to keep out beasts. Like the prickly pear, Israelis are tough and thorny on the outside but soft and sweet on the inside.

To me, the three countries in my life—my native England, Butch's homeland of Canada, and Israel—are like three daughters. England is the gentle-faced one, steady and solid. She and I have always been close. Canada is kind and gives me space to breathe, although she is more dramatic and extreme than her sister and can sometimes be icy, in both the literal and figurative sense. Israel is more mysterious, my dark-skinned daughter with the flashing eyes, exotic and potentially explosive. This daughter is so different from the other two that I wonder constantly whether she can really be mine.

Despite often challenging conditions in Israel today, Israelis are a hopeful people with a hopeful national anthem, anthem, "*haTikva,*" which means "The Hope." The words move me deeply, particularly the part that conveys that we have still not lost our hope of 2,000 years to live in freedom in a land of our own.

When I was studying Hebrew at *Ulpan* for five hours a day, five days a week over five months, we learned the words to haTikva. Our teacher wondered if they were still relevant today. "Has this goal already been achieved?" she asked.

I answered that we weren't there yet with respect to attaining freedom or the immigration of many who still hoped to come to the Land and, for whatever reason, could not do so. My basic Hebrew prevented me from saying more and, in any case, I would not have opted to do so publicly. As one who usually speaks her mind, I was often uncharacteristically silent in Israel.

My Ulpan course began in April 2010. My level aleph written exam would be in September, after the summer break. But my oral exam was before the break, in July. I was nervous.

LOVE TRIANGLES

Two ladies asked me questions. Then I told them my little *sipoor,* a story I had prepared. I said that I came home one day to find my apartment flooded. Panicking, I rushed upstairs to knock at the neighbors' door. I wanted to tell them there was a lot of water on the floor, *harbeh maim*. Instead, I told my neighbors there were *harbeh millim*, a lot of words. They looked blank. Very kindly, they came down to look regardless. Together we soon found and fixed the problem. I finished my story by saying I had made new friends through this crisis. It was a true story.

My examiners laughed in all the right places, which was reassuring. Then they asked me about my plans for my time in Israel. I said I wanted to write about biblical places, how they were then and how they are now.

Both women seemed pleased with my answer. One of them was Orthodox, with long sleeves, a long, dark skirt, and a headscarf covering her hair. As I shared my plans, the thought went through my mind, "If you only knew I want to write about Jesus, you wouldn't smile and nod."

Ideas like that served to set me apart from most of the population of Israel while I was living there. I never felt free to be myself and so I skulked around, careful not to connect too closely with anyone outside of my trusted circle, afraid they might find out I was one of those hated Messianic Jews. Ultimately, I would feel unable to sustain this masquerade.

Five years on, I have finally written about

biblical places, how they were then and how they are now, in this book. You will find here some of my meetings with Jesus all over His magnificent Jewish homeland. I have described moments I have relived from His life and tried to convey how it feels to walk with Jesus through biblical landscapes and ancient city streets. I have also written harbeh millim about the challenges other Jews and I who believe in Jesus face in Israel.

I have been amazed to discover that mainstream Jewish prejudice against Jewish believers goes all the way back to the 1st century, when early Messianics were effectively banned from synagogues by the introduction of a prayer they could not recite because it was a curse on themselves.

Judaism has not ceased to reject Jesus down through the centuries. The aspiring modern democracy of Israel rejects Him still in its policy of stripping Jewish followers of Jesus of their Judaism. That does not seem to me to be democratic. Rather, it looks more like a reversal of the Spanish Inquisition, when Jews were forced to affirm a belief in Jesus or face banishment.

Looking back, I was probably wrong in my assumptions about the Orthodox examiner. She would not have been doing the job she was if she hadn't been someone who was tolerant of people with opinions and lifestyles not her own. I suspect most Israelis were. I should not have gotten so hung up on the few still nursing archaic agendas.

But I did, right from the start.

Chapter 1 — My Secret Life

"If the world hates you, keep in mind that it hated Me first" (John 15:18).

Zafrir pointed to the spot where, as a boy, he and his father had been swimming when missiles began to hit the water around them. I looked at the sea below the promenade in Nahariya, a jaunty beach resort town near the Lebanese border, trying to imagine the alarming splashes landing around the swimmers.

"We jumped straight out of the water and made a run for it," he said and grinned at my gaping mouth and my husband's horrified expression.

Such terror was beyond our personal experience in our former lives in Canada and England. It was spring of 2010 and a peaceful time for Israel. To us, the country didn't feel war-torn at all, which made Zafrir's account of missiles seem all the more shocking.

We were *olim hadashim*, new immigrants, and Israeli-born Zafrir and his wife, Aviva, had generously opened their hearts and their home to us, inviting us to spend the day with their family. The beautiful north of Israel they had shown us had been bathed in balmy sunshine. We had found them warm people, easy to get along with. They spoke good English. Even their children did as well. The day had been a lot of fun.

As we strolled farther along the promenade, waiting for the sun to set so the trains would start up again at the end of their 24-hour halt for *shabbat*, the Sabbath, it was Aviva's turn to send tingles of fear down our spines. She told us of missiles and fighting in the north just a few years before, in 2006. She and the kids had fled farther south, to Tel Aviv to escape the danger. They had moved in with friends, stepping over one another in a matchbox apartment for what would wind up being six months, until it was safe to return home again.

Her words were rendered all the more surreal by the sun's huge ball above the Mediterranean and the sandy beach. Everything seemed so safe, but we were realizing this constant seesawing between calm and trouble had been the way of things in Israel since the beginning.

The train, when Butch and I climbed on board, was full of soldiers in camel-colored uniforms, boy and girl draftees, carrying rifles and machine guns. The line heads south, along the coast, calling at Akko, Haifa, and Tel Aviv before turning inland towards Ben Gurion Airport to terminate outside of Jerusalem. We weren't going that far today. Our

LOVE TRIANGLES

destination was Haifa, where we had rented an apartment.

We actually got to know Aviva and her children on this same train line. We had been returning from apartment hunting in Haifa to our volunteer posts in Jaffa, by Tel Aviv. They were on their way to the airport, headed for Euro Disney in Paris. The kids were bubbling over with excitement. A conversation sprang up. Aviva loved it when we told her we were olim hadashim. We were still surprised to find ourselves Israelis, like pretty much everyone else around us on that train, with healthcare and voting rights. Making *Aliyah*, as the process of immigration is called, had taken barely two months. Compare this with gaining residency for me in Canada. That had taken around twelve months, which was considered a fast turnaround.

Aviva took my cellphone number and later called me with the invitation that had led to our visit with her and her husband.

We had started our day together with a cable car ride to the Grottoes of Rosh haNikra. The British had blasted tunnels through these caves, carved out of chalk cliffs by the Mediterranean Sea, during the British Mandate years, from 1917 until 1948. The idea had been to run trains all the way from Cairo in Egypt to Istanbul in Turkey.

Today a wall of rubble marks the end of the line. Lebanon lies on the other side of it. Trains that run only south start in nearby Nahariya. There is no access north to Lebanon. The border is closed.

After out visit, we drove into Western Galilee's stunning mountains and gazed down at the picture perfect ruins of Montfort Fortress. An army from England was behind this, too, crusaders from 1,000 years ago fired with Christian zeal to annihilate the infidel Saracen and Jew.

The beauty of this country—now *our* country—took our breath away. But was it really ours?

We were joined for lunch at Aviva and Zafrir's by their South African neighbors. The wife asked me lots of questions. I felt uncomfortable, interrogated, and was cagey with my answers. It seemed like she was suspicious. I thought she might be onto me.

Was I paranoid? Perhaps.

My difficulty was that I had a whole secret life. If I told anyone I was a Jew who believed in Jesus, I risked being reviled, hated, or worse, sent away. This has happened to other immigrants who believe in *Yeshua*, the Hebrew name for Jesus.

Even secular Jews, like those we were sitting down to lunch with, who might not be expected to care what we believed, could look down their noses at us. There is a solidarity among Jews in Israel. It is not uncommon to find atheists who keep the festivals and keep kosher in their home. If nothing else, it makes it easier for a people with a vast array of shades of faith and practice to mingle. These same people can be a lot less eager to mix with Messianic Jews, who are seen as having defected to the other side.

Other faiths did not seem to have the power to

antagonize Jews in this way. The Buddhist Center in Haifa was leafleting all the apartments around, offering transcendental meditation, yoga, and other Buddhist practices. No one seemed to object.

Jewish believers associated with Messianic or Christian congregations in their home countries find their applications for immigration denied. The non-Jewish spouses of Messianic Israelis face frustrating delays and setbacks in their immigration processes.

By contrast, my Gentile husband was immediately welcomed with me and received equal immigrant benefits. Our good fortune lay in the authorities' inability to connect me with my faith. Naturally, I didn't want them to discover it and so I was careful and crept around in Israel. Meanwhile, Butch had the freedom to openly be his Christian self.

Clearly Jesus was not wanted in His homeland, except as a lure to Christian tourists. If He were a native-born citizen today, the powers that be would, no doubt, be making life as difficult for Him as they used to, like the time His own neighbors tried to throw Him off a cliff.

It happened on a Sabbath in Nazareth, which is in the Galilee region. Looking across the valleys and peaks from Isifiya, a village at the top of Mount Carmel, I have fancied that I could see the very cliff they sought to throw Him from.

Jesus had returned to His hometown, "in the power of the Spirit" (Luke 4:14). It was early on in His ministry, as "news about Him spread through the whole countryside" (v. 14). His home synagogue honored Him by asking Him to read and comment on the *Haftarah*, the day's portion from the prophets. He read from the book of Isaiah: "The Spirit of the Lord is on me, because He has anointed me to proclaim good news to the poor. He has sent me to proclaim freedom for the prisoners and recovery of sight for the blind, to set the oppressed free, to proclaim the year of the Lord's favor" (vv. 18-19).

He rolled up the scroll, returned it to the steward and sat down. All eyes were on Him as He began to teach. "Today this scripture is fulfilled in your hearing" (v. 21).

The neighbors and friends listening to "the gracious words that came from his lips" (v. 22) had trouble understanding how someone they had grown up with could really be the fulfilment of Isaiah's prophecy.

Jesus reminded them that "no prophet is accepted in his hometown" (v. 24). He said that Elijah, one of their favorite prophets, was sent to a Gentile widow rather than to his own people when they were suffering drought and famine. He reminded them there were many lepers in Israel when God led the prophet Elisha to cure a Gentile, Naaman, of the disease.

The examples He gave were not well-received. What kind of message was this, about God choosing Gentile outsiders over His own people? The people of Nazareth could hardly believe their ears. They were enraged. They grabbed hold of

LOVE TRIANGLES

Jesus and manhandled Him to the top of a cliff, intending to throw Him off. "But he walked right through the crowd and went on his way" (30).

The conclusion of this story is wondrous to me. I see it as a moment when Jesus' calm has a profound effect on those who wanted to do Him harm. They would have expected Him to struggle and pull back from the cliff edge but He knew it was not His time and He trusted God to save Him, no matter what. His demeanor totally deflated His aggressors. They let go and He passed through them and walked away.

I wish with all my heart that I had such trust. Some do. Objectors have hurled stones and smashed windows during worship at Jacob Damkani, an Israeli-born Jew from an Orthodox family and raised in a small town in northern Israel. He came to faith as a young man, while living in New York. Since that time, he has dedicated his life to spreading the gospel of Jesus in Israel and elsewhere. This has upset a lot of people.

It is said that native-born Israelis have an even harder time evangelizing than new immigrants since they are considered traitors by their compatriots. Jacob has seen churches burnt to ashes and hatred in the eyes of rioting aggressors. There have been defamatory posters and death threats. He has been attacked.

"Nazi! Nazi!" they have screamed in his face. "The Nazis burnt our bodies and you come here to burn our souls. Missionaries! Traitors! Converts!"

After their landlord buckled under intimidation and cancelled their lease, Jacob and his friends met in orchards, woods, and private homes, just like the early disciples in the book of Acts.

A Messianic congregation in Arad near the Dead Sea has suffered similarly. Gasoline has been poured around the congregation's meeting place and lit, with the intention of burning the worshippers inside. Videos of the protestors are on YouTube, but no one has been arrested for this crime. Many Messianic Jews in Israel feel the police will not protect them or their property.

Opinions among the local residents in Arad are mixed. Some say the Messianics do no harm and should be allowed freedom of worship. Others say they are not real Jews and should get out of Israel. One called them terrorists.

Shortly before my arrival in Israel, a parcel bomb, disguised as candy for the Jewish carnival festival of Purim, was sent to a Messianic family. It was opened by Ami, the fifteen-year-old son of David Ortiz, who is leader of the Messianic community in Ariel in the Greater Tel Aviv area.

It was a pretty package, the sort that are regularly sent by Jewish factions hopeful of bringing secular Jews back into the fold. When the boy opened it, the explosion threw him backwards. He lost four toes from his left foot, suffered burns, a collapsed lung, and other internal injuries. It was feared for a while that he had suffered brain damage. Thankfully, this was not the case.

The perpetrators justified what they had done

LOVE TRIANGLES

by calling Messianic Jews "Murderers of souls and destroyers of Jews."

For all these reasons, despite the kindness and friendliness of Zafrir and Aviva, I felt hemmed in.

In Israel, to declare myself Jewish would be to tell only half the story. To declare myself secular would be a lie. And to declare myself a follower of Yeshua would alienate me from the very people I longed to connect with.

With a sinking heart, I realized, as we exchanged hugs and smiles and thanks at Nahariya station and promised to do it all again, that we could not be friends with Zafrir and Aviva and their lovely children.

I loved Israel as they did. We had that in common. But I loved Jesus, too, and, although He also loved Israel, Israel did not love either of us.

Chapter 2 —What's So Special about Israel?

"Long ago the Lord said to Israel: 'I have loved you, my people, with an everlasting love. With unfailing love I have drawn you to myself'" (Jeremiah 31:3).

To me, Jesus' love for Israel shines through, first and foremost, in the beautiful imagery He used when speaking about it. When He said, "See how the flowers of the field grow. They do not labor or spin. Yet I tell you that not even Solomon in all his splendor was dressed like one of these" (Matthew 6:28-29), He was surely describing the startling red anemones that carpet large areas of the country, particularly the Negev, in early spring. He told His disciples to lift up their eyes to the barley fields in April for they were already white for the harvest (John 4:35). He spoke of Himself in this wine-growing land as the "true vine," while His Father is the gardener (John 15:1).

In Jerusalem, Jesus went often to the Mount of Olives where He could look across the Kidron Valley to the temple that His disciples described as

LOVE TRIANGLES

"adorned with beautiful stones and with gifts dedicated to God" (Luke 21:5). He loved to walk and teach in the temple courts. He participated in the Jewish festivals there. During Tabernacles, when an abundance of living water was poured over the great altar, "Jesus stood and said in a loud voice, 'Let anyone who is thirsty come to me and drink. Whoever believes in me, as Scripture has said, rivers of living water will flow from within them'" (John 7:37-38).

Although He lived simply: "Foxes have dens and birds have nests, but the Son of Man has no place to lay his head" (Matthew 8:20), Jesus enjoyed the good things of life: "the Son of Man came eating and drinking" (Matthew 11:19). His first miracle would set the agenda for the celebration of life that would follow throughout His ministry. At a wedding in Cana in the Jezreel Valley, He turned water to fine wine (John 2:1-12).

When the time came for Him to die, He showed us just how much He loved His life by asking if His Father could take this bitter cup from Him (Mark 14:36). He loved His disciples and considered them true friends. He told them, "As the Father has loved me, so have I loved you. Now remain in my love." If they did so, they would "bear fruit—fruit that will last" (John 15:9-17).

God sent Jesus to Israel and not another country because it is His Chosen Land. To Abraham and his descendants, the Children of Israel, God gave the Land of Israel, a "land the Lord your God cares for; [His eyes] are continually on it from the beginning of the year to its end" (Deuteronomy 11:12). Israel is where the Children of Israel began and where Moses led them as free men and women.

They are an example through which God shows His desire to love and bless the whole world. Through His prophets in the Land, He promised the Jewish Messiah would appear and build His church and become a Savior to all.

God repeated the promises He made to Abraham regarding Israel to his son, Isaac, and his grandson, Jacob. Jacob was given the name Israel, which means "one who struggles with God," following a spiritual wrestling match (Genesis 32). Jacob initially tried to break free, as many of us do when we are claimed by God. As the battle continued, he realized he had come face to face with the living God and changed tack, refusing to let his "opponent" go until He blessed him.

I see the ebb and flow of this fight as a microcosm of the Jewish people's relationship with their God. Since the opponent is described as "a man," perhaps we can go further still and see in this fight their battle with Jesus, God's earthly incarnation.

God sent Jesus to the Jews because, long ago, He chose them to be a holy people to Himself, a special treasure, above all the people on the earth (Deuteronomy 7:6). By so doing, He was fulfilling His promise to Abraham: "I will make you into a great nation, and I will bless you; I will make your name great, and you will be a blessing… and all

LOVE TRIANGLES

peoples on earth will be blessed through you" (Genesis 12:2-3).

Jesus claimed me during a visit to Israel in 2007, before I ever had any idea of going to live there, before I even met Butch. Marrying him was the outcome, the marvelous blessing I received from God, after accepting Jesus.

I went to Israel, saying *hineini* to God. This is Hebrew for "here I am," a phrase that comes up many times in the Bible. I was looking for something, some meaning and spirituality, after five years of sickness, including breast cancer and clots in my lungs, had left me broken. My business had failed, my long-standing marriage also.

From the beginning of my first visit to Israel, in the mid-80s, I had felt a profound sense of privilege. It would be the same every visit. There was something so special about it, as if the very air were holy, carrying on it God's murmur to me. I remember, that first time, sitting serenely on a stone wall in a small Jerusalem square, tourists milling all around me. The sunshine on my face felt like God's warm smile on me.

It was the memory of those uplifting sensations that brought me back in 2007 as a seeker. A Christian friend from Canada, Terry, met me there. We traveled the length and breadth of the country, searching, without knowing what we were looking for. Our last Sunday evening found us in a Jerusalem church, King of Kings. This was not my choice, but I felt I could not say no to Terry, who had graciously come to synagogue with me on the Friday.

The warmth and joy of the congregation hit me the moment I went in. Terry, much to my horror, began snapping photos. You wouldn't do that in a synagogue.

"This is for my brother, Butch," she said. "He'd love it here." I had never met her brother.

During the worship, I began to feel an electricity coursing through me. I felt still, calm, in the moment, and somewhere other all at once. This wonderful, godly feeling hadn't been given to me when I went looking for it in a synagogue or before a sunset but in His Son's place of worship, where I had least expected to find it.

As I sat, dazed, at the end of the service, Terry reviewed her photos. They didn't show the auditorium, the worship band, or the screen with song lyrics. They looked like tongues of golden flame. They seemed to echo what I had experienced.

I hadn't wanted to come and now I didn't want to leave. We went up together to the congregation's 24/7 Prayer Tower where, with the lights of Jerusalem twinkling at our feet, a young South African woman prayed for Jesus to receive me as His bride and, in time, to bring me a new husband of faith.

I was shocked by her prayer. As far as I was concerned, I was still only window shopping. I knew a defection to Christianity would be condemned by my Jewish friends and family and I wasn't ready for that.

LOVE TRIANGLES

There was also the fact that surgery had left me with a dire body image. I hadn't so much as dated in the two years since my marriage fell apart. A new husband was the furthest thing from my thoughts.

"What I think you need is a cloak," the South African woman said.

I was thrilled. A cloak was a very special symbol to me. I'd had a beautiful *tallit*, or prayer shawl, made up for my adult *Bat Mitzvah* that had celebrated my restoration to full health.

A cloak also appears twice in the story of Ruth in the Bible. And Ruth is my Hebrew name. The first time is when Boaz, the man of Ruth's destiny, prays to God for her protection. The second is on the threshing floor, where Ruth goes to Boaz at night.

"What do you want?" he asked, his voice still thick with sleep.

"Wrap your cloak around me," she said. By this she meant, "Marry me."

And he does.

The young woman brought a cloak of mineral green satin, the color of the Dead Sea. As I sat in the dark under its cover, all the scars from my surgeries began to ache. It was as if the dead parts of me were coming back to life.

Despite this loveliness, the shift in my life was so daunting that it took me a month or more back in my native England following my trip to accept Jesus as my Savior. But I did accept Him. And as I had anticipated, my family was upset. In their eyes, I had gone over to the other side. Still, I felt peaceful. I had so much trust in His care for me. He was speaking to me in many ways, great and small. He speaks to all who have ears to hear. All we need to do is pause in our busyness to pick up on His communications.

Shortly after I accepted Jesus, Terry received a rug in Canada she had first seen in Israel. It had taken her breath away and did the same for me when she sent me pictures.

It was a beautiful Persian picture rug that depicted a hunting scene. Pictured were four people, two women and two men. The two women were galloping towards one another on Arabian horses. They looked exactly like Terry and me. There I was with my usual furrowed brow of concentration, oval face, and wide hips. I had no doubt it was me or that the other woman was Terry.

Her search for an explanation for those inexplicable photos that looked like tongues of flame had led her to this rug on the day following our attendance at King of Kings. In a Jerusalem carpet warehouse, a Messianic Rabbi had prophesied to her that great things were on the way and the Jewish believers whose warehouse it was had shown her the rug.

The rug brought me to Eastern Canada for the first time in my life. I *had* to see it for myself. I had a wonderful, Spirit-filled visit. As it neared its end, we visited Terry's brother, Butch, the one Terry had snapped pictures for in Jerusalem. I came home from that visit and wrote in my diary that I wanted to marry this man. Terry and I had galloped towards one another on a rug and it led me to Butch, a man of strong faith, like the biblical Ruth's Boaz. We were married in September 2008, almost a year to the day after we met.

The decision to come to Israel at my time of greatest need had turned my whole life around. I was left deeply in love with the country where it all began. My hope is that one day soon, Israel will overcome its fear of Jesus. Since the 1st century, it has viewed faith in Him as a kind of leprosy among its people. It is time that changed.

A friend of mine, who we'll call Tom, believes there are ripples of a turnaround in the Land. "They are starting to reclaim Jesus from the Gentiles," he says, "and reconsider Him as one of their own kind."

His upbeat view is surprising, given the abrupt curtailment of his visa and that of his wife, Nina, by the Israeli authorities.

Their story begins with a sit-down interrogation as to their purposes the first time they entered Israel with the intention of volunteering. Although this was unpleasant, it was because they had no volunteer visa, not because they were Christian. Nevertheless, the experience left them feeling "a bit like naughty school children who shouldn't really be here at all."

In spite of the challenges, they felt God's hand in what they were doing. Soon a letter of recommendation from a government official who strongly supported their work with refugees resulted in nine-month volunteer visas. Their visas were extended by a further nine months in the fall of 2010, with multiple entries allowed. They made three or four trips in and out of Israel before going home for Christmas that year.

Their real problems began when they returned to Israel in January 2011. They found themselves being led back to the same interrogation room they'd been escorted to when they had first arrived.

There they were questioned separately. "Why are you here? Who's supporting you? Are you trying to convert Jews?"

They were not evangelizing and said as much. Even so, their passports were returned to them with "cancelled" stamped across their visas.

"We suspect that you're engaged here in missionary activity," they were told. "We are going to investigate and if, in a month, we have found nothing, you will be allowed to reapply for volunteer visas."

Evangelizing in Israel is not illegal—unless it is to minors or includes the offering of inducements to convert. In any case, Tom and Nina had not engaged in it. The most public display of their faith was to be part of the worship team during their congregation's Sabbath service.

The two were thoroughly confused. It was later hinted to them that someone had reported them, which was possible. It is thought that the authorities send spies to congregations to see who is there. However, our friends will probably never know for sure.

There was a further muddle when Tom and Nina went to their local *Misrad haPanim*, the Ministry of the Interior office in Haifa, to reapply for visas. Airport immigration had failed to communicate what had happened and, as far as the Misrad haPanim was concerned, the couple's visas were still valid.

Tom and Nina began to feel God was saying, "It's time to go home."

They decided to leave.

Despite its unexpected end, their sojourn in Israel left them as deeply in love with the Land as I am. They have great respect for the values of the State of Israel and the spirit of the Jews, in whose ways they could see God's heritage. Above all, their eyes were opened to the fact that God is in modern Israel as much as He was in ancient Israel.

Tom used to see Israel as merely "a political, rather than a God thing." His paradigm shift came in mundane circumstances, as such things often do. He was mopping the floor of the *kehilah*, the congregation building, on a Monday morning.

Asking himself what he was doing, cleaning floors in Israel rather than earning good money in front of a computer screen at home, a Bible verse popped into his head. Isaiah 2: 2 says that the mountain of the Lord's house will be the most important place on earth, raised up above other hills, and the world's people will stream to it to worship.

"A thought came to me: If you want to know the end of a story, flip to the end of the book."

He realized the Isaiah verse was describing the millennial end, with Jesus reigning over the earth from *this* Jerusalem first, before He reigns over the new earth forever from the New Jerusalem. With clarity, he saw the significance of today's Israel and how that relates to the Kingdom Come message.

"Revelation shows us Jesus reigning from Israel, from this tiny little nation in the Middle East," he told me, his voice rising.

The joy he experienced in receiving this was tempered by a sense of urgency to do something about the fact that "much of the church is off-message." Upon the couple's return to the UK, Tom began to speak widely about Israel's importance to God.

Just how widespread anti-Israeli policy is in the UK was recently brought home to me by Pamela Smith, the wife of a Methodist minister, who, in 2010, founded Methodist Friends of Israel to "bless the Land of God's everlasting covenant with His chosen people."

She has felt like a lone voice in the face of blanket condemnation of Israel by the UK media, charitable organizations, and church bodies, including her own Methodist Movement. Pamela is working for "a return to full teaching on God's relationship with Israel, past, present, and future, as revealed in Scripture."

This is a need Tom recognizes. "We could find

ourselves fighting against God, which is a horrible prospect for the church."

He and Nina now work for an international ministry that supports Jews in the Land and reaches out to the church to encourage an understanding of Israel.

Down through the centuries, likeminded Christians, many of whom never set foot in the Land, have demonstrated their support for God's purposes there. One such is CMJ, the Church's Ministry among Jewish People, for which Butch and I volunteered in Israel.

CMJ was founded over 200 years ago to help poverty stricken Jewish immigrants in the East End of London. Supported by slave trade abolition campaigner William Wilberforce and later by social reformer Lord Shaftesbury, CMJ went on to lobby for the long-prophesied return of the Jews to the homeland of their forefathers. It also offered them practical help: founding the first schools, job training programs for industry, and the first state-of-the-art hospital in the Middle East. And it built the area's first Protestant church, which still stands, looking incongruously English, near Jerusalem's Jaffa Gate

CMJ has grown into one of the biggest missions in the world, with over 250 missionaries who evangelize and support Messianic Jews as well as educating Christians about the Jewish roots of their faith.

Butch and I spent our first months in Israel at CMJ's congregation and guesthouse in Jaffa. He painted and carried out maintenance. I cooked, which I love to do. Lunch for twenty consisted of soup, a main dish, two vegetable dishes, salad, and dessert.

Beit Immanuel, the elegant former home of the Ustinovs, a famous noble Russian family, was in a state of gradual decline, like most of the neighborhood around it. Amid the crumbling Arab houses of stone and concrete apartment blocks built in the 1950s, several wooden houses that looked curiously like the older houses of New Brunswick, Canada, we had just left behind dotted the landscape.

These were the homes of a 19th century American mission bent on becoming "practical benefactors of the land and (Jewish) people." In 1866, thirty-five families from the state of Maine, USA, which borders New Brunswick, shipped homes in kit form and all their worldly goods 5,000 miles to Palestine, as the country had been known since the Romans renamed it thus in the 2nd century.

Their leader, George J. Adams, said, "We believe the time has come for Israel to gather home from their long dispersion, to the land of their fathers."

They found, to their horror, that they could not build their houses, at least not immediately. The country was then a backward and chaotic outpost of the Ottoman Empire. The contract for the land Adams thought he had bought had not yet been ratified.

LOVE TRIANGLES

There was nothing else to do but to camp on the beach while rights and permits were sorted out. In future decades, the vibrant city of Tel Aviv would grow up behind the quiet dunes where they camped, kicking off with a neighborhood of clean, white, 1930s Bauhaus properties that UNESCO has now designated a World Heritage Site.

Conditions on the beach for the colonists were harsh. This was some time before the now-ubiquitous eucalyptus tree would be brought from Australia to suck dry Israel's mosquito-infested swamps. It was grueling indeed for folk used to snowy seven-month winters to live in this hot and humid land.

The fresh springwater the Americans paid locals to bring was often drawn instead from a closer, less fatiguing but also less sanitary source. It lay immediately beside a heap of corpses, victims of a recent cholera epidemic. Within six months, twenty-two of the 157 colonists were dead.

Inexperience and sheer bad luck with the weather compounded their problems and their first harvest failed. Their leader took to drink.

By 1870 most had returned home to Maine, their zeal to help and support the Jews in God's special country spent, their cute wooden houses abandoned. The area, which lies just outside of old Jaffa's walls, is now known as the American Colony. The houses—some ramshackle, others lovingly restored—remain, a testimony to their efforts to support the establishment of a Jewish homeland.

As the Americans left, Germans arrived with similar intentions. In 1869 Protestant Templars from south Germany founded Jaffa's German Colony in a bid to accelerate the Second Coming of Jesus. They moved into the houses from Maine and built Beit Immanuel as their main office, school, and community hall. In 1904, they built the beautiful Immanuel Church with its stunning stained glass windows and its organ. Butch and I would attend worship there on those Sundays when we weren't working, Sunday being a regular workday in Israel.

We would later wind up living close to the German Colony the Templars had founded in Haifa, in a little road off the *Rehov HaGefen*, "Vine Street." The colony was a model of spit-spot urban planning—150 single-family houses with pitched, tiled roofs, shuttered windows, and pretty gardens—radiating out from a central boulevard, shaded by trees, set against a backdrop of green vineyards, climbing steeply up Mount Carmel.

The colonists, who included a remnant of diehard Americans from Maine, numbered between 300 and 750 in the years from 1870 to 1917. They farmed or followed traditional trades like blacksmithing or carpentry. They introduced modern mixed farming methods, mechanized processes, and new crops like potatoes. They developed tourism and industries like olive soap manufacturing. And they brought public transport and mail delivery to the Land.

LOVE TRIANGLES

Eventually, however, they drifted away or integrated into the local population. The First and Second World Wars saw many of them interned or deported to Australia. In Haifa, their former homes have become jaunty restaurants and shops. The houses of the Jerusalem German Colony, which was the last to be founded in 1873, now rub shoulders with Ottoman and British Art Deco architectural styles, creating an eclectic and chic residential area of that city.

The former vineyards of Haifa have been transformed into sumptuous gardens around a staircase of white terraces, intersected by graveled paths, edged with shrubs and flowerbeds. At their center is the gleaming, golden-domed shrine of the Bab, the Baha'i faith's founder. Pilgrims from all over the world converge on Haifa and on a second Baha'i holy center in the nearby ancient port of Akko. Baha'is, too, consider Israel special.

Some who have come to Israel have not done so as colonists or pilgrims but as individuals who have heard God's call on them to come to the Land. One such person was Lydia Prince. After receiving a vision of a Middle Eastern city and realizing it was Jerusalem, she abandoned a safe teaching career in her native Denmark to travel to that city as a woman alone in the misogynist world of the 1920s. The Jerusalem she came to had been torn in two by warring Arabs and Jewish immigrants.

No doubt the Arabs felt their way of life was threatened. Jerusalem is also a special religious place to them. Moslems believe the prophet Mohammed ascended to heaven from the top of Mount Zion.

In the midst of sieges, barricades, gunfire, and fighting on the streets, Ms. Prince found her purpose, which was to foster and adopt Jewish, Arab, and Christian babies whose parents' extreme poverty prevented them from raising their own children. As her biographer and husband, the late Derek Prince, pointed out, hers is a story that also catalogs the birth pangs of the nation of Israel.

The Jews fighting in Jerusalem were 19th and early 20th century pioneers with a vision of restitution of their Jewish homeland. They were eager to wipe out the label of "Wandering Jew" that had been theirs throughout almost 2,000 years of exile, ever since the Romans had carried them away from Israel in the late 1st century. All through their dispersion, they had kept Israel and its capital, Jerusalem, in their hearts, promising themselves, "next year in Jerusalem" at every annual Passover feast.

They began to farm. They launched the kibbutz system, a quasi-communistic lifestyle of shared endeavor and wealth. *Kibbutzniks* could go to the camp store and take whatever they needed—whether shampoo, snacks, or cigarettes—without having to pay. During post-Second World War austerity, this seemed like the peak of luxury. Holocaust survivors and those fleeing persecution in their own countries poured in. They built a land together, defending one another against frequent attacks. The camaraderie and love of Israel that prevailed in the 1950s are evident in the lilting, patriotic songs of the day.

During the 1960s, 70s, and beyond, hippies and others, appreciative of the commune-style way of life, poured in to help. In those days, the whole world seemed to love Israel, the gutsy young nation that was turning the desert green.

The International Christian Embassy Jerusalem was founded to counter the subsequent withdrawal of several nations' support of Israel and the closure of their embassies as the world turned. With a mission of obedience to God's command to "Comfort, comfort My people" (Isaiah 40:1), ICEJ supports Jews in the Land. The organization, which has grown exponentially around the world since its founding in 1980, also reaches out to the church to encourage an understanding of Israel's centrality to God's plans.

Aided by its supporters, Israel has become a modern day miracle. Many of these, like ICEJ and CMJ, are Christian. It is heartbreaking, but hardly surprising—given Jewish subjection to crusaders, inquisitors, and exterminators wearing Christian badges—that the Jews tend to regard that support with mistrust and suspicion.

My own daughter-in-law summed up Jewish concerns when, much to her dismay, I first came to faith in Jesus. She described a memory from her childhood: Jews for Jesus, standing on the streets of her home city of Toronto, waiting, she said, to, "steal your soul and steal your history."

Jewish Israel, an organization that takes a critical look at Israel's alliances with Christian groups and monitors evangelical campaigns directed at Jews, believes the "overwhelming political and economic support for Israel which comes from the very same parties which have and continue to target Jews for conversion has confused Jewish leadership and blurred the line between friend and foe."

There is a budding recognition that Jews and Gentiles who love Israel need to work together to melt the hearts of hardline Jews like those in charge of the Misrad haPanim and Christians who condemn Israel as the aggressor as it fights for its very survival.

The seeds of a new closeness would seem to lie, in part, in shared adversity.

"This summer looked more like 1938 than 2014," Ron Lauder, President of the World Jewish Congress, said in his keynote address to ICEJ's 2014 Annual Conference, referring to a year when 120,000 Christians were killed in the Middle East and Africa and many more were made refugees as anti-Semitism all over the world also rocketed.

He called for a new unity. "I am now convinced we must join forces. A Jewish-Christian coalition makes complete sense."

His words were met with hearty applause from his Christian audience, whom he reminded, "There is no safer place in the Middle East for Christians than here in Israel."

God's chosen land is not only safe for

LOVE TRIANGLES

Christians but truly evocative. A huge element of Israel's specialness to Christians is how easy it is to meet Jesus there, under that sun, in that landscape, surrounded by Middle Eastern architecture, plants, trees, and wildlife.

Chapter 3 — Where the Bible Comes to Life

"How beautiful are your tents, Jacob, your dwelling places, Israel!" (Numbers 24:5)

Butch and I have watched demonstrations of biblical carpentry in a reproduction of Jesus' workshop in the Jesus Village in His hometown of Nazareth. The carpenter's shop would have been *the* place where news and views would be exchanged with customers while they waited for their repair or piece to be made.

It was exactly that way for Butch in 2010, when they needed a new door for a bathroom at work.

"I know a carpenter in Nazareth," his boss said and off they drove, reaching the Nazareth carpenter's shop in well under an hour. It had hinged wooden doors that were pulled back, opening the shopfront to the street where Arab shoppers in ankle-length robes headed to and from the market. As if living out the Bible, Butch and his boss waited and chatted, while their door was made.

LOVE TRIANGLES

Did Roman soldiers ever come to Jesus' workshop? I wonder. If so, might they have ordered crosses for crucifixions from Him? Maybe so. The Romans would appear to have been in Nazareth: what is thought to be a Roman bathhouse, a beautiful, high-vaulted room with an underfloor heating system, was discovered by a Christian Arab and his Belgian wife during renovations to their souvenir shop and home in the 1990s.

Recently, archaeologists have suggested that a 1st century house of mortar and brick cut into the stone cliff face is probably the very one where Jesus grew up. Both Byzantine Christians and Crusaders are thought to have accepted that this was where Jesus was raised. A church decorated with mosaics, built over it, has served to help preserve the structure.

Ancient houses remain all over Israel. On a Jaffa street undergoing road construction, we saw the shape of one emerge out of the red earth. It had a flat roof like that on which the disciple Peter had a vision while taking a noon nap at the house of Simon the Tanner, also in Jaffa (Acts 10). Such roofs were accessed via a ladder or steps. Grass would grow on them during winter and would have to be cut down in spring so that the family could sit out and enjoy the cool breeze of evening and sleep under the stars on beds that would be rolled up and stowed away in the morning.

The next day a desk and chair had appeared beside the house and a female archaeologist sat taking notes. A few days later all trace of it was gone; it had been recorded and covered over.

In Jerusalem is the Burnt House. Burned at the time of the destruction of the temple, it may have stood at the time of Jesus' crucifixion, forty years before. Certainly houses very much like it would have existed then.

The house is in an area once popular with priestly families who served in the temple. A round stone about four inches across was found inside, inscribed with the words *Bar Kathros*—"Son of Kathros"—indicating that it probably belonged to the Kathros family. This family is mentioned in the *Talmud,* the Oral Law, as priestly producers of incense for the temple. Jugs, bowls, and measuring vessels found in the house support the idea that a perfume-producing workshop existed here. Intriguingly, the Talmud reports that the Kathros family abused their position.

Was Nicodemus, a member of the Jewish ruling council who became a follower of Jesus, a neighbor of the Kathros family? Perhaps he knew them. Maybe Jesus did too and debated points of the Law with them at the temple. If they did not know one another personally, the chances seem strong that they would have heard of one another since, within the high, thick, gray stone wall encircling Jerusalem, around 25,000 people lived in an area of just one square mile.

How many manufacturers of perfume were there in town? Could the woman who lavishly poured perfume from an alabaster flask over Jesus' head have purchased it from the Kathros family? Might she even have been a perfume maker herself? It was women's work. Samuel warned the people of Israel that if they opted to have a king, he would "take your daughters to be perfumers" (1 Samuel 8:13).

That the Kathros family was wealthy is demonstrated by their house. The traditional Israelite home on display at Tel Aviv's *Museum haAretz* shows us the type of house most common in biblical times. It had three rooms of modest proportions and would generally be built of mud and straw. There is no doubt that the Burnt House, consisting of four rooms, a courtyard, a kitchen, and a *mikvah* used for ritual immersion, was luxurious by Jewish standards. The presence of a personal *mikvah* supports the contention that the owners were a priestly family. The cement outer walls of the Burnt House would have been covered with a thick white plaster. The floors were of beaten earth, with sunken ovens of clay set in them.

In the kitchen of the Burnt House, a stove, a grinding stone of basalt for milling grain and pressing olives, and stone jars have been found. This stone kitchenware further points at priestly occupation because a household strictly observant of Jewish law would have preferred stone to pottery. Items found inside more modest houses have generally been made of clay. These include pots, plates, lamps, fish hooks, weights for fishnets, striker pins, and weaving bobbins.

The courtyard of the Burnt House was paved with stone, a further luxury. Whenever it was warm enough, which was a large proportion of the year, cooking and almost all other activities would have been undertaken there. Courtyards often included a shady fig or pomegranate tree to supplement the family's fruit supply. A wooden gate in the high surrounding wall would lead to the street.

None of this came close, however, to the opulence of certain Roman houses of Jerusalem and Caesarea, with their mosaic floors, tinkling-fountained entranceways, and manicured gardens surrounded by columns and *trompe l'oeil* wall paintings.

As fire-scorched wooden beams, walls, and ceilings of the Burnt House collapsed during the fire, the contents were covered with debris and a layer of ash and soot that preserved them. Scattered fragments of stone tablets, ceramic and stone vessels, iron nails, shelves, furnishings, ink wells, oil lamps from the Roman period, and other household objects have been recovered.

Bones of a woman approximately twenty-five years old have also been discovered as well as an iron spear she may have brandished against the Romans.

The house also had a tunnel that covered drainage. These were common in Jerusalem during the Roman period. The 1st century historian Josephus wrote that Jewish rebels hid in such tunnels from the Romans.

LOVE TRIANGLES

At the end of the Roman siege of rebellious Jerusalem—when many had died of starvation and those who remained had resorted to gnawing on leather belts and stuffing tufts of grass into their mouths—the Roman soldiers entered the city with, according to Josephus, "joyful acclamations for the victory they had gained . . . Seeing nobody to oppose them . . . they went in numbers into the lanes of the city with their swords drawn. They slew those whom they overtook without mercy and set fire to the houses whither the Jews were fled, and burnt every soul in them, and laid waste to a great many of the rest . . . and made the whole city run down with blood, to such a degree indeed that the fire of many of the houses was quenched with these men's blood."

The Romans were swift and heavy-handed to put down uprisings, and Jerusalem was not quiet in Jesus' time but filled with hatred of them and smoldering resentment against their occupation. Jesus' own story illustrates how violent it was. He was not crucified alone. Neither was He the first to undergo such horrific punishment.

It would seem that Jerusalem, city of faith, is still a city of hatred. Beyond extremist terror attacks, I sensed an underlying mistrust and dislike for one another among the Jewish and Arab populations. For instance, a Jerusalem storekeeper, who kindly offered to drive us up to take a look at the Mount of Olives, was visibly anxious when he did so. His concerns seemed validated when some Arabs, crowded together in a small car, asked him pointedly what he was doing there.

We didn't stay very long.

Another time I enquired about training as an official tour guide and the convener threw into the conversation that half the class would be Arabs.

"So?" I said, not understanding why she was making this point.

"I had to mention it," she replied. "Many Jews refuse to train with them."

I hadn't been in Israel long enough then to understand the deep pain that each side feels for its losses. The horrific experience of the son of the minister at Beit Immanuel while serving in the Israel Defense Forces will serve as an example. He saw his friend gunned down at point blank range as the two of them checked the IDs of Arabs coming into Jerusalem to work. The assassin drew a gun instead of his ID, lifted it to the boy's temple, and in a flash, he was gone.

Haifa, where I lived, seemed calmer and a lot more tolerant, although, as we shall see later, it has not been immune to trouble. It is not somewhere we know Jesus went, although He was raised in nearby Nazareth and, during His ministry, visited Tyre and Sidon, coastal towns a little to the north, which would have looked quite similar. Yet I would often fancy He fell into step beside me when I walked there, which I loved to do.

Haifa sits on the slopes of Mount Carmel. Carmel means "God's vineyard orchard, or garden." My favorite walk would take me steeply

LOVE TRIANGLES

uphill to the Stella Maris church. Inside, it is as pretty as a frosted wedding cake. Tourists mill around it and the funicular car across the road. I always chose to walk down the mountainside towards the shimmering Mediterranean rather than ride.

My path passed crumbling, scrubby terraces. The stones that supported each level could have been from biblical times or a mere century old. I could not tell. An 1825 contributor to the *New Monthly Magazine and Literary Journal* paints a picture of how these slopes once looked: "No mountain in or around Palestine retains its ancient beauty so much as Carmel. Two or three villages and some scattered cottages are found on it; its groves are few but luxuriant; it is no place for crags and precipices or rocks of wild goats but its surface is covered with a rich and constant verdure."

There may not be "crags of the wild goats" (1 Samuel 24:2) like those surrounding the Dead Sea, but we have seen goats feeding on foliage in the forest at the summit of Mount Carmel. We have also seen hyenas and heard jackals. Downtown, in a park, I have seen the alarming earth churnings made by wild boar.

In such a hot country, the "rich and constant verdure" would have been a special feature of this area throughout time. In spring, 3,000 years or a mere handful of decades ago, the terraces before me may have been filled with barley ripe for the picking, with wheat for the wealthy ripening alongside. There may have been orchards of pomegranate and olive trees, flax and vegetables such as leeks, garlic, cucumbers, red and green peppers, eggplant, melons, dates, legumes, and herbs.

Or perhaps there were vineyards stretching as far as the eye could see. The parable about a vinekeeper in Isaiah 5 tells us a great deal about what good vineyards looked like: neatly pruned vines across fertile hillsides cleared of stones. Perhaps they were walled against marauders with narrow paths between the walls, like the one Balaam's talking donkey "pressed close to, crushing Balaam's foot against it" when an angel appeared on the path (Numbers 22:24-25).

In Song of Songs, the beloved invites her lover to go to the vineyards with her in the spring, to see if the vines have budded and their blossoms have opened. "The pomegranates may also be in bloom," she says (Songs 7:12). Perhaps they will smell the heady scent of mandrakes.

By July the vines would have been heavy with bunches of grapes beneath the vineyard watchtower. Nearby, hewn from the bedrock, would have been a winepress where the grapes would be trodden and turned to juice.

All produce required constant tending. Workers in the fields would have fetched water, and merchants, leading their asses and mules on their way to market, would have bartered and loaded up that produce and tied it up alongside pots and bolts of fabric.

LOVE TRIANGLES

Leaving my picture of a pastoral idyll on the terraces, my walk would descend, via a stone staircase under cooling, tangled trees, to Elijah's Cave. Elijah, one of the greatest Jewish prophets, is associated with the Carmel area. On the other side of the mountain, facing the broad Jezreel Valley, a beautiful garden marks what is thought to be the spot where he once brought down God's holy fire to overcome Queen Jezebel's pagan priests of Baal.

Elijah's triumph would signal the end of three years of drought. He looked for a sign of this until, at last, a single cloud appeared like a fist above the sea. It grew and finally, the skies opened to release torrential rain.

The skies above my apartment kitchen overlooking the Mediterranean were surely that spot. They seemed wondrous to me and always busy. One time I watched billowing clouds head in from the north and south simultaneously to meet above my kitchen. How could this be and what would happen when they collided? To my surprise, they broke up into little speech bubbles that floated gently out towards the water.

Such curiosities are really not so curious in a country where the very breeze seems to carry on it the whisper of God.

Elijah's Cave, at the foot of Mount Carmel, is said to be where God spoke to Elijah as he hid from Jezebel, who was trying to kill him. "The Lord said, 'Go out and stand on the mountain in the presence of the Lord, for the Lord is about to pass by. Then a great and powerful wind tore the mountains apart and shattered the rocks before the Lord, but the Lord was not in the wind. After the wind there was an earthquake, but the Lord was not in the earthquake. After the earthquake came a fire, but the Lord was not in the fire. And after the fire came a gentle whisper. When Elijah heard it, he pulled his cloak over his face and went out and stood at the mouth of the cave" (1 Kings 19:11-13).

It seemed to me that such a momentous holy experience couldn't have happened in the place they called Elijah's Cave, with walls that today are dark and toxic from the fumes of trucks and vehicles passing noisily along the coastal highway. A curtained barrier the length of the cave separates the male prayer area from the female. I neither heard nor felt God there and rarely went inside.

My walk continued along the seashore on the opposite side of the highway, passing derelict buildings beside the sands. The rundown beach at *Bat Galim*, which means "Daughter of the Waves," did not match its romantic name. A lovely beach with enticing restaurants a mile or two outside of the city was where we would go to swim.

Just south of it is Caesarea, with its wonderful remains of Herod the Great's Roman seaport. There I fancied I met Peter as he evangelized the centurion Cornelius and his household. Under instruction from God, received in Jaffa during the vision already mentioned, Peter set aside his

LOVE TRIANGLES

kosher diet to make this happen. I imagined them all reclining in the painted *triclinium*, the Roman dining room, and the slaves bringing the Roman delicacy of dormice on silver trays. Poor Peter's face would surely have been a picture then.

A stele that mentions Pontius Pilate has been discovered at Caesarea. Perhaps he had a weekend home there. The sea breeze that would blow through the rooms would have been a welcome relief from the intense summer heat of the overcrowded alleyways of Jerusalem.

In Caesarea Paul was tried and imprisoned. This gave him plenty of time for thinking through his theology and writing it down in the form of letters. The instruction we might have been deprived of, had he not been held in this way, seems to me to be a demonstration of how God works His purposes out through apparent adversity.

My return home from Bat Galim would take me past a naval base, the Rambam Hospital, and the German Colony's restaurants. The everyday hubbub of Israel—the buses, cars, and pedestrians—always brought home to me that everything in Jesus' time seemed as everyday to Him and everyone else as all this had become to me.

In Israel, the ancient past merges with a present made up of high tech and avant-garde, Coca Cola and McDonalds. Modernity is a thin veneer over a Middle Eastern underbelly. While a million plus Russian immigrants have wielded sufficient influence to teach Israelis how to stand in line and wait their turn, they have also brought vodka and drunken states that were previously almost unheard of.

Eating my sandwiches outside the hospital following a fasting blood test one time, I found myself in the midst of Arab men in dishtowel headdresses and long robes and ultra-Orthodox Jews in black knickerbockers and hats all rubbing shoulders in an everyday manner.

While the Arabs were dressed like biblical Jews, the Jews were dressed like 19th century Europeans. I imagined a *minyan* of the Jews, ten men, the minimal number required for communal prayers and rituals, sitting around a big, wooden table covered in dusty scrolls and books to dispute what Hillel said versus Shammai's pronouncements or those of some other long-dead, learned leader.

The place for such debate is a *yeshiva*. *Yeshivot,* plural, are where Talmud and *Torah,* the first five books of the Bible, are studied. Yeshivot existed way back, before the time of Jesus. The apostle Paul studied under Rabbi Gamaliel the Elder, grandson of the great Hillel, at what would have been a yeshiva.

With clarity I imagined Jesus joining a yeshiva, at least for a few days. In Luke 2:41 we learn that when He was twelve years old, His family went up to Jerusalem for Passover, as they did every year. This must surely have been His *Bar Mitzvah.*

After becoming Bar Mitzvah, which means "Son of the Commandment," a Jewish boy is considered a fully-fledged member of the community of Israel. The ceremony is a time of song, dance, and joyful celebration, for the boy is now a man who can be called upon to read Torah portions in the synagogue and fulfil other duties such as making up a minyan.

Joseph and Mary would have brought Jesus to the temple to read the portion He had prepared from the Torah scroll. I have seen fresh-faced Bar Mitzvah boys at the Western Wall, which is all that remains today of the Jerusalem temple, carrying Torah scrolls and wearing their first adult tallit, or prayer shawl, just as Jesus would have done.

What might His portion have been? Something special from Exodus for the Passover? We can only wonder. Nowadays synagogues get through all the Torah portions in a Jewish year. Back then it took them three years to go from the beginning of Genesis to the end of Deuteronomy, which, incidentally, was the duration of Jesus' ministry.

As young Jesus began to deliver a *drashah,* or "commentary," on His portion, the priests would no doubt have been astounded by His knowledge and perception, all the more remarkable since He was a country boy with a provincial Galilean accent. Here was someone who would normally be expected to follow his father's trade rather than throw Himself deep into the Scriptures.

After Passover and all the celebrating were done, Jesus' party set off for home. Dangers on the open road meant there was safety in numbers. Psalm 22 says, "Rescue me from the mouth of the lions; save me from the horns of the wild oxen." Bandits and thieves like those who set upon the man the Good Samaritan helped were a further hazard. Friends, neighbors, and relatives from Nazareth would have traveled together in large numbers. This was why Jesus wasn't missed until evening.

When Joseph and Mary discovered He was not with them, they rushed back in a panic, climbing again up steep Mount Moriah, this time against the flow of pilgrims who would have been pouring out of Jerusalem. They climbed to the very top, perhaps entering via the north side of the city, the only side that did not contain deep ravines, or from the road up from Jericho that bridged the Kidron Valley. They spent the next three days searching for Him, becoming increasingly frantic.

Perhaps some in Jerusalem had already heard about the young luminary from out of town and directed His parents to the yeshiva He had joined. Following His Bar Mitzvah, the priests would have wanted Him to stay, perhaps even offering Him a scholarship at a prestigious temple yeshiva. That was where His parents found Him, calmly debating biblical texts with learned men, "sitting among the teachers, listening to them and asking them questions" (Luke 2:46).

Instead of expressing their heartfelt relief, Jesus' parents were furious.

"Son, why have you treated us like this?" His mother said. "Your father and I have been anxiously searching for you."

LOVE TRIANGLES

Jesus replied, "Didn't you know I had to be in my Father's house?" (vv. 48-49).

I used to think that was the punchline and point of this story, a demonstration that the temple was Jesus' Father's house, which took precedence over everything else. But that cannot be it, I realized, because Jesus gives it up and goes with His parents.

I think what we are actually being shown is Jesus' reaction to the realization that He is the Messiah. What better time and place for this knowledge to come to Him than at His Bar Mitzvah at the temple?

If God opened Jesus' eyes at that moment to His destiny of becoming our High Priest, a title attributed to Him by the writer of the book of Hebrews, then joining a temple yeshiva would no doubt have seemed the most logical step to start on that path.

His parents' wish for Him to come home with them turned all that around however. God's commands through the Ten Commandments told Him to honor His father and mother. He saw that it was His Father's will that He comply with their wishes and return to Nazareth with them.

In this way God made it clear to Jesus that He did not want Him to be a scholar but someone with real life experience. No doubt young Jesus wondered how a carpenter from Nazareth could ever become High Priest. He already knew, however, that God's ways were greater than those of man. Nothing was impossible for God.

Told this way, the story becomes one of epiphany: God shows Jesus the kind of Messiah He is to be, a man of the people.

I wonder also whether Jesus, looking into his adoptive father Joseph's eyes, saw death lurking there. This is the last time we hear of Joseph in the gospels. In the event of his death, Jesus, as the eldest, would have been responsible for raising his half brothers and sisters, the children of Mary and Joseph.

Exploring Bible stories in a deeper way, as I have done here, is a favorite occupation of mine. It has been a favorite occupation of rabbis—and their students at yeshivot—since time immemorial. This practice is called *midrash,* which means "what results from investigation."

Midrash puts flesh on the barebones stories of the Bible. Given that vellum, the animal skin on which the sacred scrolls were written, was expensive and time-consuming to make, after which followed the slow task of copying out the text, it is hardly surprising that Scripture was written with great economy.

Midrash enlarges upon a core story, taking it in different directions and adding embellishments, hopefully plausible ones. Some of these have become so commonplace within Judaism that most Jews would be hard put to tell you which parts of a tradition are biblical and which have been passed down orally.

I was pretty sure that many of those ultra-Orthodox Jews smoking their cigarettes outside the

LOVE TRIANGLES

hospital alongside their Arabic neighbors wouldn't be able to make the distinction. Although perhaps, like me, they saw the Bible coming to life everywhere they went, I was also pretty sure that, unlike me, they were still waiting for the Messiah to come.

Chapter 4 — Still Waiting for the Messiah

"He asked, 'Who do you say I am?' Simon Peter answered, 'You are the Messiah, the Son of the living God'" (Matthew 16:15-16).

On the third day of the war that would become known as the Six Day War, Israeli forces made it all the way to the Western Wall in Jerusalem, their most holy place. Because of the oceans of tears Jews had shed down through the centuries, praying ardently for their return to the Land, it was better known at that time as the Wailing Wall.

There the Chief of Chaplains of the Israel Defense Forces, Rabbi Shlomo Goren, sounded the *shofar*. His triumphant notes on the curling ram's horn trumpet reverberated through the twisted alleyways of Jerusalem's Old City.

It was June 7, 1967. For almost twenty years, since May 1948, when the State of Israel came into being, Jerusalem had been a divided city. The rubble of the flattened Jewish Quarter and its synagogues had lain like fallen fighters, following Israel's birth. Barricades, barbed wire fences, and a scrubby strip of no-man's land had separated the Jews from their beloved Wall and the rest of the Temple Mount.

"We have taken the city of God," Rabbi Goren declared. "We are entering the Messianic era for the Jewish people, and I promise to the Christian world that what we are responsible for, we will take care of."

Rabbi Goren's promise to Christians affirmed the undertaking of the State of Israel to safeguard the holy places of all religions. Jews and Christians share the Old Testament holy sites. The New Testament sites are important only to Christians because they concern Jesus, the Jewish Messiah the Jews do not recognize.

Just why did Rabbi Goren say they were entering a Messianic era? Can it be that the Jews now believe the end of their long wait is at hand?

The Bible prophets say the first requirement for the Messiah's coming is the return of the Jewish people to their land.

They had returned after the Babylonian exile in Old Testament times and been exiled once again, carried away by the Romans. Jewish history is viewed as cyclical rather than linear. So Jews are not surprised to see prophecies fulfilled—and then fulfilled again. Since the 1800s, after almost 2,000 years of dispersion, they had been coming back into the country. Nazi Germany caused droves more to pour in throughout the latter part of the British Mandate. The British detained them behind barbed wire in camps or sent them back. After

1948 these immigrants became free citizens of the new nation of Israel and the floodgates were opened for Jews to return to their ancestral homeland.

This first Messianic trigger having been fulfilled, Rabbi Goren was hailing the restoration of Jerusalem as the second vital step ahead of the coming of the Messiah, as foreseen by the prophets.

As well as returning the Jewish people to their homeland and restoring Jerusalem, Jews expect the Messiah—a title meaning "anointed one," in the same way that high priests and biblical kings were anointed with oil—will rebuild the temple and re-establish temple practices. The Temple Institute in Jerusalem is already preparing for this by recreating temple treasure replicas such as the magnificent, solid gold, seven-branch candlestick that stands on public display near the Western Wall.

The problem is that the stunningly beautiful Dome of the Rock, a sacred place to Moslems, stands on the former site of the Jewish temple and has been there for well over 1,000 years. The Dome marks the spot from which Moslems believe their holy prophet, Mohammed, ascended to heaven. It is the self-same rock Jews believe bore the altar on which Abraham prepared to obediently sacrifice his only son, Isaac, in a demonstration of faith in God's promise to him that his descendants would be as numerous as the stars.

At the last minute God saved Isaac, instructing

LOVE TRIANGLES

Abraham to sacrifice a ram instead. Abraham could have had no inkling, as he stood with his knife raised above his son, that God was making the point, through this event, that He alone would sacrifice His Son.

A thousand years before Christ, Solomon's temple, a place of worship and atoning sacrifice for the Jews, would be built on this same rock. The second temple, built by Herod the Great, stood at the time of Jesus. His once-and-for-all atoning sacrifice on the cross removed the need for a temple to make atoning animal sacrifices. Jesus' disciple John saw no temple in the New Jerusalem "because the Lord God Almighty and the Lamb are its temple" (Revelation 21:22).

Some prophecies, such as the closing chapters of Ezekiel, appear to suggest that there will, even so, be a temple during the Millennium and that sacrifices will be made there. However, the building of a third temple looks most unlikely as long as the Moslem Dome of the Rock stands on Mount Zion. So it would appear there is no completion of the Messianic era in sight as foreseen by the Jews.

A further difficulty arises from the expectation that the Messiah will be of David's line. Since the genealogies of the Jewish population were kept in the temple and it was destroyed by the Romans barely a generation after Jesus' death, it is now impossible for anyone to establish descent from King David with any degree of certainty.

Gospel writers Matthew and Luke would have had access to these records since they were writing before its destruction. The lineages they give demonstrate that Jesus was of David's line, both through His mother, Mary, and His adoptive father, Joseph.

The Messiah the Jews are expecting will not only be descended from King David but, like him, will also be a man of great faith and devotion to God, a great leader, and a judge who makes righteous decisions. He will be a warrior who restores Jewish self-respect and national pride. He will redeem his people, spiritually and politically.

The apostle Paul's greatest evangelical challenge in the synagogues was to prove that Scripture pointed to a Messiah who would also suffer and rise from the dead. "'This Jesus I am proclaiming to you is the Messiah,' he said. Some of the Jews were persuaded . . . but other Jews were jealous; so they rounded up some bad characters from the marketplace, formed a mob and started a riot in the city" (Acts 17:3-5).

These poles-apart reactions to the message of Jesus as the Messiah are still current among Jews today. Jesus is not what they have always expected. A shift in thinking is necessary. Confirmations that Old Testament texts considered trustworthy point in the direction of Jesus, the surprising Messiah, make the shift easier. This was what Peter, like Paul, did in the book of Acts, as well as Philip when he witnessed to an Ethiopian slave and Stephen when he addressed the Sanhedrin. They provided the sort of evidence that would bring Orthodox Jew, Jacob Damkani, to faith as a young man in New York in the 1970s.

Since Jews are expecting the Messiah to be a man and not supernatural in any way, they find the Christian belief that Jesus is the Son of God abhorrent. In the time of Jesus, deification of human beings was a practice of the hated pagan Romans. The strength of their feelings is illustrated by a New Testament story about Herod Agrippa, King of Judea and grandson of Herod the Great.

Luke is the author of Acts. His disdain for Herod Agrippa's social climbing is plain as he describes how first, he left his kingdom for grandiose Caesarea and stayed there instead of returning home to do his job of ruling Judea. Then, when Gentiles from Tyre and Sidon came to make peace following quarrels with him, he received them sitting on his royal throne in his royal robes and with a display of virtuoso Roman rhetoric that was intended to dazzle. Duly impressed, or at least wishing to appear so, they shouted, "This is the voice of a god, not of a man!"

"Immediately, because Herod did not give praise to God, an angel of the Lord struck him down, and he was eaten by worms and died" (Acts 12:22-23). The moral here is that any man who accepts the title of god will be punished by the Lord. It is where the Jews still stand today.

Yet Isaiah's description of the Messiah as "Wonderful Counselor, *Mighty God*, Everlasting Father, Prince of Peace" (Isaiah 9:6) (emphasis mine) demonstrates the Jews *should* expect their Messiah to be God. There are Jewish websites that try very hard to refute this prophecy by translating it differently. However, the Hebrew Bibles I have consulted translate Isaiah's Hebrew expression *El Gibbor* as Christian Bibles do, with the term "Mighty God."

The Dead Sea Scrolls, discovered in a forgotten cave just one year before the founding of the State of Israel, confirm there was a 1st century expectation that the Messiah would be the Son of God. Scroll 4Q246 says, "He shall be called the Son of God, and they shall designate him Son of the Most High," which sounds a lot like Luke 1:32, "He will be great and will be called the Son of the Most High."

The idea of a father and son can sound like two gods. Judaism stands firm that there is only one God. The *Shema,* the closest thing Judaism has to a doctrine, says, "Hear, O Israel: the Lord our God, the Lord is one" (Deuteronomy 6:4). Jews despised those Romans who venerated many gods and they deplore Christianity as a polytheistic faith with three gods. I know I once thought this way too.

Now I understand there is only one God in Christianity, and it is the same one as in Judaism. He has three aspects: the all-powerful Father Omnipotent, the Son Incarnate, made flesh, and the Holy Spirit Immanent, who dwells within us. Jesus confirmed He was one with the Father in John 10:30.

He said this when asked at the temple whether He was the Messiah. It was *Chanukah*, the Jewish festival that focusses on a miracle of light. Jesus' response was that the miracles He performed and the eternal life He promised His followers confirmed who He was, but none of it would ever be enough to convince his questioners. The Messiah they expected was more like Judas Maccabee, the hero of the Chanukah story, who successfully led a revolt against the Syrian Greeks who had been oppressing Jewish religious practices.

Looking back, I don't know why I found it so hard to see that God could have three aspects, given that my Old Testament God was already a God of aspects. His very name in Hebrew, *Elohim*, is plural. Genesis 1:1, strictly translated, should read, "In the beginning, Gods (plural) created (singular) the heavens and the earth."

Jews also believe in the *Shekinah*, considered to be the presence of God, sometimes called His glory. The pillar of cloud by day and the pillar of fire by night that guided the Children of Israel away from slavery in Egypt are God's Shekinah: "The cloud covered the tent of meeting, and the glory of the Lord filled the Tabernacle" (Exodus 40:34). In temple times, the Shekinah dwelt in the Holy of Holies. I was actually taught by a feminist rabbi that the Shekinah was the "feminine aspect" of God.

We also find the *Ruach,* or "Spirit." It was there at the creation, for example, hovering above the face of the waters in Genesis 1:2, and it was upon Moses and the elders he appointed in

Numbers 11:16-29.

Not all Jews share the same expectations about the Messiah. The Reform Movement of Great Britain, to which I used to belong, rejects the idea of a personal Messiah, a new temple, and the restitution of its sacrifices. Instead, it embraces the concept of a Messianic Age, when swords will be beaten into plowshares and man will study war no more (Isaiah 2:4). In this world to come, there will be no crime or poverty but peace on earth. It is unclear what the Reform Movement sees as the trigger for this Messianic Age.

Although I accepted these ideas at the time, I now see that rejecting an individual Messiah rode roughshod over many predictions in the *Tanach*, the Old Testament, regarding His identity and coming, of which I was previously unaware.

Orthodox Jews, who expect an individual Messiah, are sure He will come before the year 6,000 in the Jewish calendar, which is 2230 of the Common Era. The year 6,000 will be the first year of a Sabbath millennium, the seventh since the creation. *Kabbalah*, the study of ancient wisdom aimed at understanding how the world works, says that the seventh millennium will be a 1,000-year Sabbath. Just as the seventh day of the week is the Jewish Sabbath day of rest, the seventh millennium will be 1,000 years of universal rest.

The concept of a Messianic era lasting 1,000 years is echoed in Revelation. "Blessed and holy are those who share in the first resurrection . . . They will be priests of God and of Christ and will reign with him for a thousand years" (Revelation 20:6).

Christians look to a Second Coming of Jesus Messiah. In Luke 21 Jesus predicted many shakings prior to His return, including wars and threats of wars, natural disasters, persecution of His followers "on account of my name" (v. 12) and signs "in the sun, moon and stars" (v. 25).

All of this seems to be in process already in our present day. The outcome Jesus promised is that we shall see "the Son of Man, coming in a cloud with power and great glory. When these things begin to take place, stand up and lift up your heads, because your redemption is drawing near" (vv. 27-28).

He will come to Jerusalem, to the Mount of Olives, east of where the temple once stood, as Ezekiel foresaw. "The glory of the Lord entered the temple through the gate facing east" (Ezekiel 43:4).

The conflict in Jerusalem that, sadly, is still ongoing is central to the predictions Jesus made. "When you see Jerusalem being surrounded by armies, you will know that its desolation is near" (Luke 21:20). "This is the time of punishment in fulfilment of all that has been written" (Luke 21:22).

In Sandhedrin 98A of the Talmud, we also find predictions of shakings ahead of the coming of the Jewish Messiah. Rabbi Johanan foresaw, "A generation overwhelmed by many troubles as by a river . . . When the enemy shall come in like a flood, the Spirit of the Lord shall lift up a standard against him." Then the Redeemer will come to Zion.

Jews and Christians agree that our Redeemer will "pour out on the house of David and the inhabitants of Jerusalem a spirit of grace and supplication." At that time, we will all look upon the One that we have pierced and "mourn for him as one mourns for an only child, and grieve bitterly for Him as one grieves for a firstborn son" (Zechariah 12:10).

Before the return of the Jews, Jerusalem languished; it was a dormant backwater part of the world. It is their return that is keeping it front page news and is carrying us towards the fulfilment of both Old Testament prophecies and those of Jesus. Israel's vigorous policy to open its arms wide to all Jews who want to come home. However, it is coldly turning its back on one category of Jew— those who accept Yeshua as their Redeemer.

Chapter 5 — Jews Who Believe in Jesus Not Welcome!

"Do not be afraid, for I am with you; I will bring your children from the east and gather you from the west. I will say to the north, 'Give them up!' and to the south, 'Do not hold them back.' Bring My sons from afar and My daughters from the ends of the earth—everyone who is called by My name, whom I created for My glory, whom I formed and made" (Isaiah 43:5-7).

"Your children and wife also want to make Aliyah?" the Israeli Consular official of a US city asked my friend. We'll call him Ben.

Ben nodded. He and his wife, Melissa, exchanged smiles. They had been dreaming of making Israel their home for a long time.

Aliyah literally means "going up," a term originally used to describe how Jews from all over the ancient world would go up to the temple at the very top of Mount Zion in Jerusalem for Jewish pilgrimage festivals.

"Where do your children go to school?" the official asked.

Ben gave the name of the local Christian academy they attended.

The official shifted in his seat. "Tell me," he said, "are you a Christian?"

Cheeks burning, Ben mumbled something about his wife being a Christian.

The official looked at Melissa and back at Ben. "It is not a problem if your wife is a Christian. But if you are a Christian, Mr. Green, that is a big problem. So what is your faith?"

Ben hung his head, knowing he was cornered. Ben was Jewish, Melissa a Gentile. Both believed in Jesus. He would not deny Christ, but to acknowledge Him would mean the end of their dreams. He said nothing.

"Look," the official said, shuffling the papers in front of him, "your application will almost certainly fail if you are a Christian. Would you like to take your check and papers away and think about it?"

Ben and Melissa took their application home and ripped it up with heavy hearts.

The original Law of Return, passed in 1950, gave all Jews the automatic right to citizenship in their Jewish homeland. Amendments excluded convicts and those representing a health hazard. In 1970 Aliyah rights were extended to the children and grandchildren of Jews, irrespective of whether their Jewish ancestor was male or female. This new egalitarian ruling ignored the tradition that Judaism is passed down through the mother's line.

LOVE TRIANGLES

The law was also expanded to include full rights for the non-Jewish spouse or partner of Jewish immigrants. In 2014 this ruling was tested to discover whether it included same-sex couples. It does.

The State rabbinate, which controls marriage and divorce, does not permit gay marriages within the Land but recognizes those conducted abroad. They are exactly the same conditions that apply for heterosexual Jews marrying non-Jews. Several young Israeli colleagues at the Messianic congregation where Butch and I worked were obliged to go to Cyprus or Spain to wed their Gentile fiancés.

The legal difficulty Ben came up against was the interpretation of the Law of Return 1970 Amendment 4B. This reads, "For the purposes of this Law, 'Jew' means a person who was born of a Jewish mother or has become converted to Judaism and who is not a member of another religion."

Ben could have declared himself an atheist and been welcomed in with open arms. But not a Messianic Jew.

Almost all cases dealing with Aliyah have to go to the Supreme Court of Israel. This is because, historically, the whole issue of Aliyah has been considered so important that it was put under that court's jurisdiction. The court is so busy that cases may drag on for years. Long waits can lead to cases being dropped by plaintiffs who would rather get on with their lives, an outcome that is no doubt welcomed by the powers that be.

Israeli lawyer Joshua Pex, himself a Messianic believer, told me that in the early days, things were far less rigidly defined than they are today. There weren't many believers. Joshua's parents, Judy and John, who have never made a secret of their faith, were welcomed in as immigrants at the same time as appeals over Aliyah aimed at establishing that Jews who believed in Jesus were still Jews were failing.

One such was the appeal of Gary and Shirley Beresford against their rejection which was considered a landmark case because they were strictly observant Orthodox Jews. The couple had lost family members in the Holocaust and had close connections with Israel through relatives already living there, some of whom had founded a kibbutz. They believed in Yeshua as their Jewish Messiah but were not practicing and had not joined a believer congregation. They continued to observe Levitical Law.

"The court could have said, 'Okay, you're Messianic Jews, but we still see that as part of Judaism,'" Joshua pointed out. "But they did exactly the opposite."

Woven throughout the judgement that was handed down was a theme of separation and becoming other, the idea that Messianic Jews had cut themselves off from the Jewish people. The judges referred to the reaction by mainstream Judaism to the very early believers.

As we learn in the book of Acts, the first

decades of Messianic evangelism consisted almost exclusively of Jews like Paul, Barnabas, Silas, Timothy, John Mark, Philip, and Peter himself reaching out to the network of synagogues across the Roman Empire. Some accepted their message. Others did not like it. Peter was arrested in Jerusalem more than once and faced execution. Paul's message caused riots among Jews living beyond Israel's borders. They beat him and left him for dead.

Jews who accepted Yeshua as their Messiah faced expulsion from the synagogue, which translated as shunning by the whole Jewish community. This was a big deal. We find an example of it during Jesus' lifetime as Pharisees investigate the healing on the Sabbath of a man born blind.

When the man's story was checked with his parents, they were reluctant to answer questions beyond confirming that their son was born blind. This was "because they were afraid of the Jewish leaders, who already had decided that anyone who acknowledged that Jesus was the Messiah would be put out of the synagogue" (John 9:22).

When the previously blind man attempted to defend what Jesus had done for him, "they threw him out" (John 9:34).

The issue the Pharisees had—and mainstream Judaism still has—is summed up in an accusation synagogue leaders levelled against Paul as he evangelized: "This man," they complained, "is persuading the people to worship God in ways contrary to the Law" (Acts 18:13).

By the end of the 1st century, believers had been forced out of synagogues everywhere by the addition of a new prayer that they could not say for they would be cursing themselves. It did not mince words but cursed the "renegades" and asked that the "arrogant Nazarenes and the *minim*" might "perish and be blotted out from the book of life." The Nazarenes were those who followed Yeshua the Nazarene and the minim were most likely *ma'aminim*, which means "believers."

You would think the traditional Jews could have found a stronger insult than "believer." Many Jews were said to have entered concentration camp gas chambers singing *"Ani ma'amin,"* a reference to Maimonides' Thirteen Principles of Faith, which says, "I believe with a full heart in the coming of the Messiah, and even though he may tarry, I wait for him on any day that he may come."

In the end it would be the Nazarene believers in Yeshua who would walk away from mainstream Judaism. This happened during the Jewish Bar Kochba Revolt of the 2nd century, which they supported until leader Bar Kochba was hailed as the Messiah by the famous Rabbi Akiva.

There has been no reconciliation between traditional and Messianic Jews since.

Orthodox Jews have ignored and, if all else failed, besmirched the name of Jesus. The Talmud's few references to Him are mainly slanted and derogatory. Medieval Jewish writings, though they neither deny Jesus' existence nor His miracles, explain them as trickery and present Him as a charlatan and a liar.

Things are not that different today. When I told my former husband that I had accepted Jesus as my Savior, he exclaimed, "That imposter!" He didn't know the first thing about Him and was even under the impression that He was a minor prophet in the Tanach. Yet he had his strong opinion.

In certain places the number of Jews who believed in Jesus is thought to have been high but, like myself, they have felt the need to keep their faith a secret from other Jews rather than risk exclusion by their own people in an anti-Semitic Christian world.

The landmark case that first defined the modern State of Israel's position regarding Messianic Jews was that of Brother Daniel in 1962. After the Ministry of the Interior refused to grant him Israeli citizenship on the grounds that he was a Christian, Brother Daniel took his appeal to the Supreme Court. There he declared, "My religion is Catholic, but my ethnic origin is and always will be Jewish. I have no other nationality. If I am not a Jew, what am I? I did not accept Christianity to leave my people. It added to my Judaism. I feel as a Jew."

Surprisingly, the Chief Rabbinate was on his side. They ruled that the priest, born to Jewish parents, should be granted citizenship as a Jew.

"The Supreme Court decided that if you are a Jew who believes in Yeshua, you are not a Jew any more in terms of the Law of Return," Joshua Pex said. "You are a member of another religion."

Under Justice Moshe Silberg, the Court decided 4-1 against Brother Daniel, stating that, by converting to Christianity, he had cut himself off from his heritage.

He still had the right to attain citizenship through naturalization, however, and this is what he eventually did. Brother Daniel headed up the Carmelite Monks in Haifa until his death in 1998. His was an extraordinary life.

Born Oswald Rufeisen in Poland in 1922, he became a member of Akiva Youth, a pro-kibbutz Zionist movement. As the Nazis rolled into Poland at the start of the Second World War, he fled east to Vilna, Lithuania, where he survived the Soviet takeover and was able to obtain a visa to send his younger brother out of Europe. The brother went to Israel and became a farmer on a collective farm near Haifa.

When the Nazis invaded Lithuania, Rufeisen was made a slave laborer. However, he managed to escape with papers stating he was a Christian. Crossing the border into White Russia, he came to Mir where, speaking both German and Polish, he talked himself into a job as translator for the German military police

He used his position to smuggle police arms to Jews in the ghetto at Mir. Overhearing a phone conversation that the ghetto was about to be liquidated, he tipped off the Jews, who escaped while he created a diversion. His action saved nearly 300 Jewish lives. Disguised as a nun, he continued saving Jews throughout the War. In 1945 he converted to Christianity and changed his name to Brother Daniel.

After the War he identified war criminals and testified against them. Post 1948 he wanted to fight for Israel in the Arab-Israeli War. His only way out of Poland was to renounce his Polish citizenship. This he did and came to Israel in the 1950s.

If such a Jewish hero as this could be refused citizenship, what hope could there possibly be for other Messianic Jews? How was it that I got in?

After Butch planted the idea in my mind, I tentatively checked out whether we qualified. Inspirational and moving videos of families and individuals making Aliyah on the website of an immigration agency in Jerusalem did their intended job of firing me up with patriotism. That wasn't hard. I already loved Israel. They also convinced me that here was a place where Butch and I would be able to build a life together.

One sunny January day we took the bus from Tel Aviv in our t-shirts. Jerusalem was overcast and cold, but the agent was friendly and welcoming. He didn't ask us about our beliefs. He confirmed we qualified to make Aliyah.

I came away from that meeting with my fear of staying gone. What Butch had sparked had grown into a strong desire in me. I really wanted this. It was as if a long-suppressed dream, an idea that had seemed fanciful because it was so overwhelming, could become reality if the two of us were in it together.

Even so, when we handed over our completed application and documents on our second visit, I was jittery. Our designated agent almost pounced on our marriage certificate to scrutinize it. This was the make or break document. No doubt he was looking to see whether I'd married my Christian husband in a church, which I had. But all it stated was that we were married in Fredericton, New Brunswick. Clearly embarrassed by his display of fervor, he explained it away by telling us that he was a former public registrar with a particular interest in marriage certificates from all over the world.

Though I was happy to have gotten over this hurdle, I felt kind of sneaky. It was like I was posing as someone else because I fell short of some required standard. Over time that feeling would become a nagging itch I couldn't get rid of.

Now that our own application was in, our friends at Beit Immanuel where we were volunteering, though overjoyed that we wanted to stay, told us we would likely be checked out and should distance ourselves from their Messianic congregation. We rented an apartment in Haifa owned by friends from my former synagogue.

On March 15, 2010, the day of our interview, we were at the bus stop before 8:00 a.m., even though our appointment was not until 12:15 and the journey should not take more than three hours. However, three hours later, our bus was stuck at a

LOVE TRIANGLES

standstill on *Kwish 6,* the arterial toll highway that links Haifa to Jerusalem. From our seats at the front, a long line of halted cars stretched into infinity.

We would later discover that this was the day the rebuilt Hurva Synagogue would be dedicated. Razed to the ground by the Arab Legion during the War of 1948, it was the first new synagogue in Jerusalem's Old City since that time and everyone was on high security alert. Roadblocks were everywhere.

I prayed for the panic that was bubbling up inside to leave. Suddenly calm filled me. "For I know the plans I have for you, plans for good and not evil" (Jeremiah 29:11) came into my head. God had things taken care of, just like He did all along. He picked me up and gave me faith and blessed me.

I smiled at Butch and told him all would be well. "We can surely do this," I said, echoing the words of Caleb, one of my biblical heroes, from Numbers 13:30.

Eventually we got close to the roadblock as the traffic inched forward. Every vehicle was being inspected. We got through it only to snake our way slowly up the mountainside to Jerusalem in more congested traffic. We took a cab from the bus station, when usually we would walk, and arrived at the agency's office around 12:30.

Joy! The officers of the Mizrad haPanim had also been delayed. They had only just arrived from Lod. We were offered apologies for their lateness and invited to enjoy hot drinks and a spread of pastries. It had been ages since breakfast, but I was too nervous to eat much. As I nibbled on a croissant, I wondered what questions they would ask me.

As it turned out, they didn't ask us anything. The officiating women were all smiles. They put the standard form under my nose. I had no problem confirming that I was not a member of any other religion because I had no affiliation to any congregation of any persuasion at that time. We even had to remind them that Butch was not Jewish when they gave him the same form to sign. It was totally okay for him to belong to any religion he liked.

"Welcome to Israel!" our agent said, steering us towards his office after we'd signed the forms.

"You know you'll have to serve in the Army now?" He grinned at Butch who looked taken aback. "Don't worry, though. All you'll need to know is the Hebrew for 'run' and 'duck' and you'll be fine."

There was laughter all round.

A week later, we each received our *Teudat Zehut,* our beautiful Israeli ID cards. It really was official. We were in and it had all been so easy.

Butch and I celebrated with a day out at Zichron Yaakov, a cutesy, quaint town just south of Haifa. It is perched above the Mediterranean, with pretty architecture, a winery, artisans, and boutiques. Sitting on a terrace under a jaunty umbrella and watching the diamond sparkles of the warm April sun on the sea below, I experienced a balmy, laid-back feeling.

This was now our home.

We called Butch's sister, who was more or less living in Jerusalem on back-to-back three-month tourist visas that she would renew through "visa runs," short trips to somewhere close, like Cyprus or Jordan. We didn't tell her our news—not just yet. She wouldn't be pleased that we had waltzed in, attaining what she could only dream of.

Terry was one of the many with "Jerusalem Syndrome," the name given to people of any faith who have an overwhelming desire to make the holy city their home. Many seem to be Jewish wannabes like her, Christians within Israel and without, eager for a stake in the Land of the Bible.

Ken and Sadie, an American hippy couple who came regularly on three-month evangelical stints, wanted nothing more than to live in the Land. DNA tests had confirmed their Jewish ancestry, but the State of Israel is not currently recognizing DNA profiling as proof of Judaism except for Jewish orphans whose parentage is uncertain.

Solomon, originally from South America, told me, "My Aliyah journey goes back hundreds of years, as my father's family is *Anusim* Jews from Catalonia, Spain. We were forced to either leave Spain or convert."

The descendants of these converts, known as *B'nai Anusim*, may be convinced they are Jewish but cannot prove it. They cannot make Aliyah.

Laura, who is from the States, believes she

has a similar history to Solomon. "I am a Benjamite by ancestry," she explained, "but I'm Christian. Obviously my ancestors, possibly through the Spanish Inquisition, dropped Judaism."

The Spanish Inquisition was in 1478. I asked her how she knew she was Jewish.

"My husband suggested we try DNA testing," she told me. "We did and I was blown away. I found that my ancestry is from Israel, probably around 3,000 years back. I have mainly Benjamite blood, with a little Judah, which is pretty typical."

Benjamin and Judah are two of the original twelve tribes of Israel. It is thought that large numbers of Benjamites were exiled to Spain by the Roman Emperor Titus in the 1st century. This remains speculative history that cannot reliably be confirmed by DNA testing, however much Laura would like it to be so. Nonetheless, she is content.

"Having been a Christian since my early teens," she said, "it has made a massive difference to me to know I have roots in the faith I love so dearly."

Solomon, who until recently was practicing Messianic Judaism, said, "I'm the first in my family, both in Europe and America, who has returned to the community of Israel after the Inquisition, and trust me, as we speak, Jews of Spain are returning to the community of Israel."

I asked him why, in light of this, he was having such trouble establishing his Jewishness.

"I'm a Jew in America but not in Israel," he replied. "It depends who you ask."

LOVE TRIANGLES

"Does Israel now accept you as Jewish?" I asked on learning that he was associating with rabbis there.

"Not the Ministry of the Interior, no."

If he wants that to happen, he will have to formally convert. Some nominally Christian Anusim feel that is a bit much to ask, since their problems were caused by being made to convert in the first place. Others would not even consider conversion for it would mean denying Christ.

With DNA testing only establishing strong possibilities rather than hard data and origins lost in the mists of time, it is difficult to see how the Ministry could have any way of discovering who, of those calling themselves Anusim, really are.

Like Solomon, my friend Simcha has had a lot of trouble with the Ministry of the Interior. She moved to Israel from the UK in 2011 along with her family. Simcha always knew she was Jewish. Clearly, she told me, other people knew it too and didn't like her because of it. She remembers a big boy ordering her to go back to "Jew Land" when she was just a little girl.

At thirteen, a family history project brought home to her the atrocities her relatives had suffered during World War 2. Her grandfather's back was broken during the Holocaust and he was left paralyzed until he became a believer, at which point, Simcha told me, "He was healed and walked fine again for the rest of his life." He is named at *Yad VaShem*, the Holocaust Memorial Museum in Jerusalem, as one of the Jews saved through the efforts of Swedish diplomat Raoul Wallenberg.

When Simcha was still at school, an Orthodox Jewish classmate told her, "Our call is to live in Israel. We should be there."

Simcha felt that call. Before leaving the UK, a rabbi she checked with assured her she was Jewish. She, her Gentile husband, and their children came to Israel expecting Aliyah to be a formality.

"We threw ourselves into life here," she told me. "We found an apartment, set up our bills and taxes and put our roots down. So imagine our surprise when we were told that our application had been denied."

She was told her Christian baptism and wedding meant she was no longer Jewish in the eyes of the State of Israel. Her protests were to no avail. She got legal advice and reapplied for citizenship, this time as the granddaughter of a Jew.

A three-year wait followed, during which time her husband was allowed to operate his self-employed business from Israel. But the family paid higher taxes than other residents and "an absurd amount for healthcare." When baby number three came along, they had to pay for a private homebirth.

Their new son had no status in any country, but the Ministry of Births, Deaths, and Marriages took pity on them and issued him with an Israeli birth certificate. It had no ID number or any registered parents but, fortunately, was sufficient to get him a British passport.

Meanwhile, the Mizrad haPanim missed deadline after deadline. Almost every month they asked for a further extension.

"We struggled with understanding what God was doing," Simcha said. "We knew we were in the right place. He had spoken very clearly to us about planting us deeply into the land, but we didn't understand why we needed to go through this."

Without any kind of visa, they felt they could not leave the country for fear they would not be allowed back in.

"After about eighteen months, I remember saying to my husband, 'What better way to plant us in the land than to stop us from leaving!'"

In Simcha's mind, going back to the UK was never an option. "We never wanted to give up. That is something miraculous."

Finally the family received an offer of two years' temporary residency. This should subsequently result in the granting of permanent residency.

"This gives us virtually all the same rights as a new immigrant. We get the ID and the healthcare and the taxes are adjusted. We can live like anyone else."

If permanent residency ensues as they hope, they may, like Brother Daniel, later apply to become citizens. The switch-up is not always straightforward. When, after thirty-eight years of permanent residency, Joshua Pex's father, a Gentile Dutch national, applied for citizenship, the process took a lot longer than it should have, no doubt due to characteristic delaying tactics by the Ministry of the Interior. In the end, the Ministry wanted to interrogate Joshua's American-born mother, Judy, who had been an Israeli national for decades. They asked her about the Shelter, the guesthouse she and her husband have in Eilat, on the Red Sea.

"It's a regular hostel," Judy told them. "We have people from all over the world."

She didn't mention that many of their guests are Christians.

"What kind of religious activities do you have?"

"We have *Kabbalat Shabbat*," she said, omitting that their Sabbath celebration is Messianic.

The battle Simcha has been through has left a bitter aftertaste. Her family won't get the blue passports she feels she has a right to and won't ever be recognized as Jewish. The process she has been through has stirred up questions about who she is and whether she has been mistaken her whole life in identifying herself as a Jew.

She deplores the lack of understanding officials have displayed for the circumstances of European Jews who have undergone conversions, mixed marriages, and, she says, "many other heartbreaking attempts to hide their identity. That doesn't change our identity. The Nazis would have considered me Jewish."

She is also angered by what she sees as Israel's massaging of worldwide sympathy for its

LOVE TRIANGLES

Holocaust victims while operating a policy that denies some of their descendants' rights. She considers the Ministry of the Interior unnecessarily mean.

"It was like they knew they couldn't deny me, but they didn't want to succumb. Offence has been given."

Simcha is now putting her struggle behind her. Deep down she says she knows that Israel, "a place that accepts God's call on it," is right for her.

American friends of ours, Mike, who is a Jewish believer, and Linda, his wife, a lifelong, churchgoing Christian, may run into similar difficulties when they apply to make Aliyah, which is their intention. They have sold their big house and downsized to a condo near a major US airport with direct flights to Tel Aviv.

We got to know them in Israel. They have been on several trips to see whether they liked it. After deciding they did and needing a reference from a rabbi for their application, they began attending a Reform synagogue since Mike's family, growing up, was attached to the Reform movement. The rabbi there encouraged their Aliyah plans until, one day, looking perplexed, he showed Mike an article about Mike and Linda's most recent trip to Israel. It suggested they had gone there to evangelize. They had not and Mike was able to emphatically deny this. He is uncertain to this day how the local publication sourced its story.

The rabbi seemed satisfied. Nevertheless, Mike

and Linda worry that this article may compromise the application for Aliyah they intend to make. "Will the Misrad haPanim interviewer ask as about our respective faith and religion in the land of democracy and alleged religious freedom?" he wonders.

A big question brought to the fore by the way the Ministry implements the Law of Return that the Supreme Court upholds is whether Jewishness is a race or a faith. Historically, it has been thought of as both.

Today the State of Israel, like other modern states, strives to separate faith and government in society. It faces an uphill struggle because the Orthodox community strongly resists all forms of what it sees as the secularization of Judaism in Israel. It lobbies hard against citizenship rights for Jews following other religions, and, as we have seen, it will also not allow Jews to marry non-Jews in the Land.

This leaves the government in an uncomfortable position, with policies that echo in reverse the restraints once placed on the religious freedom of European Jews: today, Jews must not be Christians if they want to move to Israel.

The Supreme Court has judged they have abandoned their Judaism. But are Messianic Jews really Hebrew Christians or are they following a branch of Judaism?

Attending and working for Messianic congregations in Israel, I found fundamental differences from Gentile Christian practice and belief. Places of worship are called *kehilot*, congregations, rather than "churches" and you will never see a cross in one.

I used to think this was due to the unfortunate symbolism of the cross, which was once featured on the tabards of murdering crusaders and is representative of a Christianity that has burned, expelled, forced conversion upon, led pogroms against, and ultimately sought the Final Solution, the extermination of the Jews.

The absence of a cross does not imply that the crucifixion and resurrection are denied or ignored. They are not. Yeshua saves us to eternal life. But the focus in Messianic Judaism is considerably more weighted towards His being the fulfilment of ancient prophecy and towards the rich Jewish symbolism of His every word and gesture. The emphasis is very different from that of most churches I have attended. Christianity has traditionally ignored the Jewishness of Jesus, focusing instead on His ministry, often to the virtual exclusion of the whole of the Old Testament after the Fall of Adam and Eve.

Messianic Judaism, out of which Christianity grew, continues to celebrate all the Jewish festivals and the teachings of the Tanach, linking Messiah Yeshua to each of these, as indeed He Himself did. The faith and practice developed directly out of the traditional Judaism He practiced. Messianic Jews continued to circumcise, keep kosher, and keep Shabbat, as numbers of Gentile believers, excused from these Jewish aspects of faith, grew.

Eventually there were many more of them than of the original Jewish believers. Messianics have not converted to Christianity but are "completed Jews," in that the Messiah they were awaiting has come. This is the only real difference between their Judaism and that of other observant Jews.

In defining Messianic Judaism as "another religion," the Supreme Court of Israel is depriving the faith of an element of the richness of its own diversity. In making the Supreme Court responsible for such definitions, the government manages to avoid being more explicit legislatively about what the Law of Return means. It sidesteps the necessity to make a clear decision about the question of who is a Jew. The government distances itself further from any responsibility for the issue by appointing Ministry of the Interior operatives, who make decisions based on the Supreme Court's rulings.

"If you hint at any connection to Christianity," Joshua Pex said, "they will do everything they can to make things difficult for you."

Meanwhile, the government takes pains to demonstrate that its citizens are not required to accept any religious dogma. You can be granted citizenship even if you are hostile to Judaism. So long as a rabbi confirms you are a Jew or the child or grandchild of one, you have the right to become an Israeli. It seems they believe Jewishness is in the blood.

But the admission of converts seems to confirm that Judaism is a faith. And the way the

LOVE TRIANGLES

1970 Addendum to the Law of Return is currently interpreted, rejecting Messianic Jews as Christians, looks that way too.

So I guess it's still both, even if the State of Israel seems somewhat befuddled about the question.

Joshua Pex told me that the judges could revise their thinking at any time and overturn previous rulings. Handing down his judgement in the Beresford case, Judge Barak, who would later become Chief Justice of the Israeli Supreme Court, said, "*At the moment,* being a Jew who believes in Jesus is not part of Judaism."

"He left it open," Joshua said, "that, in the future, things could change and the ruling could change."

For that to happen, however, there would need to be a shift, either in the way the facts are viewed or in the culture. There seems little prospect of that in the current climate.

"In practice, from what we see, it's not going to change anytime soon," Joshua confirmed. In his view, things are actually getting worse.

He told me about a new Aliyah application form with all the normal questions plus one around what form of Judaism the applicant practices. Messianic Judaism is on the list. Anyone ticking that box will quickly find their application refused.

While some might give themselves away in the assumption that Messianic Judaism has become acceptable, those in the know face a dilemma: Is not ticking the box tantamount to denying your faith?

More significant than the sly trickery that the form employs and the soul-searching it seeks to provoke is the undeniable fact that, if it lists "Messianic Judaism" as an option under a question about the branch of Judaism practiced, this is an admission that it is a branch of Judaism and not of Christianity.

Isn't it?

Hardline Jewish attitudes to what is seen as the defection of their own to Jesus are still the order of the day. They were what almost ruined Ben and his family's plans to make Aliyah.

Despite the rejection they had experienced at the Israeli Consulate in the US, they prayerfully decided to bite the bullet and, like Simcha and her family, showed up in Israel. Things went much more smoothly for them there.

Totally committed to the success of their endeavor, they sold everything before leaving the USA. Given the difficult economic conditions at that time, they thought it might take a while to sell their house. To their amazement, it sold within two weeks.

The Consular Officer's suggestion that they take their application away with them proved a further blessing. They arrived in Israel label-free and their applications to stay were accepted without question.

They are now an Israeli family. Their daughter, Ashley, is serving in the Israel Defense Forces, an obligatory two-year stint for all girls from the age

LOVE TRIANGLES

of eighteen, and their son, Danny, is about to start his three years of service.

Clearly God was in their plans all along, as He was in our own.

Chapter 6 — This Year in Jerusalem

"If I forget you, Jerusalem, may my right hand forget its skill, may my tongue cling to the roof of my mouth if I do not remember you, if I do not consider Jerusalem my highest joy" (Psalm 137:5-6).

 For us the Jewish promise to be "Next year in Jerusalem" at *Pesach* was this year. Here we were, along with thousands and thousands of other Jews and Christians, visiting from all over the world to celebrate Passover and Easter. Sometimes the dates do not coincide. Passover, which lasts for a week, begins on 15th Nissan, a date that varies according to the Jewish lunar calendar. Easter, on the other hand, falls on the first Sunday after the first full moon after the spring equinox.

 In Jesus' day, Jerusalem would have been just as busy. Passover was one of the three big Pilgrimage Festivals, the other two being *Shavuot,* or Pentecost, in the late spring, and *Sukkot*, which is Tabernacles, in the fall. Jewish pilgrims included, "Parthians, Medes and Elamites; residents of

LOVE TRIANGLES

Mesopotamia, Judea and Cappadocia, Pontus and Asia, Phrygia and Pamphylia, Egypt and the parts of Libya near Cyrene; visitors from Rome (both Jews and converts to Judaism); Cretans and Arabs" (Acts 2:9-11).

Whether native Israelis or foreign Jews, all needed to sacrifice a lamb at the temple to remember the blood of the lamb that was daubed on the doorposts of the Israelite slaves in Egypt. This blood saved them when the angel of death passed over them.

It was no coincidence that Jesus' crucifixion and resurrection took place at Passover. Like the Paschal lamb, He was sacrificed to save us from death. Like Moses, who brought the children of Israel out of bondage to freedom, and whose story is told at Passover *Seder* meals by Jews everywhere, Jesus leads those who follow Him into the Promised Land of redemption.

Butch and I were headed to the Garden Tomb, a couple of blocks from the Damascus Gate. We walked through a heaving Arab market in the Old City that serves the daily needs of the local population. It was full of colorful and fragrant displays of vegetables, spices, fish, bread, freshly roasted nuts, and baklava, a Middle Eastern dessert made of filo pastry and chopped nuts, soaked in honey. There were also practical items like bowls and pots and pans but almost none of the souvenir trinkets that abound elsewhere in the Old City. The Damascus Gate market felt authentically biblical. It put us in the mood for some time travel.

The tomb is real and ancient with a stone that would have been rolled across the entrance, as was the way in the time of Jesus. The garden is comprised of olive trees, sycamores, flowers, and birdsong. It may not be the actual one where they laid Jesus. Apparently the Church of the Holy Sepulcher has the stronger claim. The Emperor Constantine's mother is credited with discovering Christian holy sites like the Holy Sepulcher in the Land. I'm not a fan of this church. It's very dark, with a depressing atmosphere, a monument to division within the church where denominations compete: Greek and Russian Orthodox go this way, Roman Catholics that, to see Calvary.

The Garden Tomb, on the other hand, is somewhere to feel how it was when it all happened.

Next to the peaceful garden was a cliff face that, today, overlooks a bus depot. Many Arabs were walking along the sidewalk in traditional dress. Despite the bustle, I felt contemplative. The cliff face looked like a skull. Surely this was Golgotha, "the Place of the Skull," where Jesus was crucified?

We were due north of the temple here. Passover lambs were sacrificed by the Northern Gate of the temple, where the great altar stood. It was fitting that Jesus' sacrifice should be oriented the same way they were towards the Holy of Holies.

After His excruciating death, His most

influential and secret followers, Joseph of Arimathea and Nicodemus, claimed His body and laid it on the slab inside the tomb. "Nicodemus brought a mixture of myrrh and aloes, about 75 pounds" (John 19:39). Josephus, the ancient historian, boasts that 40 pounds of spices were used to prepare the body of the famous Rabbi Gamaliel the Elder. So 75 pounds, possibly half Nicodemus' weight, is a huge quantity, demonstrating how respected Jesus was by these men.

"Taking Jesus' body, the two of them wrapped it, with the spices, in strips of linen. This was in accordance with Jewish burial customs. At the place where Jesus was crucified, there was a garden, and in the garden a new tomb, in which no one had ever been laid. Because it was the Jewish Day of Preparation and since the tomb was nearby, they laid Jesus there" (John 19:40-42).

What a terrible day "Nicodemus, the man who earlier had visited Jesus at night," (v. 39) had! His teacher had been put to death in a most humiliating way. As a religious leader, Nicodemus would have known full well the verse from Torah that said, "Anyone who is hung on a pole is under God's curse" (Deuteronomy 21:23).

His own Passover was ruined. Instead of taking a lamb to the temple to be slaughtered for his family's Passover celebration, he had instead, sought out, bought, and hauled vast quantities of spices and linen for Jesus' burial. The wrapping had to be hurriedly done because all work had to be finished before the Sabbath.

By involving himself in the burial, Nicodemus rendered himself ritually unclean. Exposure to death is the most extreme form of ritual impurity. This is not because death itself is dirty—or even spooky. It is contact with the absence of God-given life. By his actions, he debarred himself from taking any part in the Passover.

Just east of where Butch and I stood gazing at the skull on the face of the cliff, large flocks of sheep would have grazed at the edge of the wilderness before the Passover. On the day of Jesus' death, their bleating would have quietened, becoming as if muffled by the dramatic drop in their numbers as they were purchased and led away to the temple for slaughter.

What remained was close-cropped grass that the rains had made lush for spring and the flapping awnings of the tents of the shepherds who brought them to Jerusalem from various parts of the country, including nearby Bethlehem. "Follow the tracks of the sheep and graze your young goats by the tents of the shepherds," the Daughters of Jerusalem told the Beloved (Songs 1:8).

With great care, each family selected a male lamb or kid, one year old and without blemish, and took it to the temple. Only those who were circumcised and ritually clean were allowed to take part in the sacrificial ritual, which usually took place at 3:00 p.m. on the afternoon before the start of Passover but would have been at 2:00 p.m. on the day Jesus was crucified since the

LOVE TRIANGLES

Sabbath was coming in and work would cease as it did. It is a relatively rare occurrence for the eve of Passover to fall on the Sabbath.

Jesus' sacrifice was completed at the same time as that of the thousands of sacrificial lambs would have been. Three hours of strange darkness preceded His death. So the slaughter would have taken place in an eerie blackness. The priests may have needed to light torches in order to see. At about 3:00 p.m., "Jesus cried out in a loud voice, *'Eli, Eli, lama sabachthani*?' (which means 'My God, my God, why have you forsaken me?') . . . He gave up his spirit" (John 46-50).

He had been led, as Isaiah prophesied, "like a lamb to the slaughter" (Isaiah 53:7).

His final words were the first line of Psalm 22, a psalm that is amazing in its detail surrounding the circumstances of His death. Since people of the time knew scripture by heart in the same way that many of us today know the words to songs or famous lines from movies, they would immediately have understood what Jesus was pointing them to.

An earthquake serious enough to damage the temple followed. "At that moment the curtain of the temple was torn in two from top to bottom. The earth shook, the rocks split and the tombs broke open" (Matthew 27:50-52).

Some scientists are suggesting precise dates, April 32 or 33 CE, for the crucifixion, based upon earthquake evidence. A comparison between Dead Sea seismites within laminated mud of a known 31 BCE earthquake and that of a second major earthquake appears to confirm that the second earthquake took place around 31 CE, give or take five years. Any attempts at more precise dating look to me like pseudo-science.

When I tried to date the Passover of the crucifixion, I also got nowhere. Thinking how cool it would be if the resurrection took place on the same date I was claimed by Jesus in Jerusalem, which was Sunday, March 25, I tried to find out when Passover was in the years surrounding the possible date of His death.

Exodus 13:4 simply says Passover is to take place in the month of Abib, the first month of the ancient Hebrew calendar. In those days, months were not fixed as they now are and the high priest could discern a date for Passover based on how advanced the crops were.

Our attempts at calculation have been further muddied by an 18th century switch from the Julian to the Gregorian calendar, when we all jumped forward in time eleven days.

What we can be sure of is that, as Jesus suffered on the cross, participants in the Passover were lining up with their beasts in the temple court, waiting their turn. Before them, long lines of priests, each holding a gold or silver cup, reached all the way to the altar. These cups had rounded bottoms like scoops, that would not stand if you set them down. Their shape helped prevent the blood from coagulating, which was not desirable.

The gates of the temple court were closed and the sacrifice began. Levites, standing close by, sang the *Hallel*, Psalms 113 to 118, to the music of brass instruments.

Only a priest was permitted to catch the animal's dripping blood, although a layman might do the killing. The cups containing blood had to be passed quickly back along the line, before it could coagulate. The priests nearest the altar sprinkled the blood on the altar. They handed back empty cups to the front to catch the blood of the next beast.

Each animal was hung up on hooks and skinned. The fatty portions intended for the altar were cut from its abdomen. These were placed in a vessel, salted, and offered by the priest as the remaining entrails were taken out and cleansed.

There were three successive groups of participants. When the ritual was complete for the first group, the temple court gates were opened and the second group took their place, then the third.

Participants would carry their lambs home to roast on spits made of pomegranate wood. They took great care not to break any of the animal's bones, neither during the cooking nor the eating. None of Jesus' bones was broken during His crucifixion either. Though the Roman guards intended to break His legs, they found He was already dead and so did not bother. "These things happened so that the Scripture would be fulfilled: 'Not one of his bones will be broken,'" (John 19:36).

The lamb would be eaten at the evening meal.

Participants would recline, leaning to the left, like Roman freemen, a Passover tradition that persists to this day. Everything had to be eaten that night. No leftovers could remain until morning. The Seder, or "order," that accompanied the meal told the Exodus story, the Jewish journey from bondage to freedom.

How badly were they shaken at 3:00 p.m.? Was any of this feasting still possible?

Did Nicodemus walk home through streets fragrant with the alluring smell of lamb roasting on open fires a dejected and isolated man with silent tears streaming down his face as folks all around him celebrated into the night with wild delight?

Or were they picking their way, distraught, through debris after running in all directions from the temple whose columns were keeling over? Were escaped lambs wandering, braying, in every direction as Jesus was laid in a stone cold tomb?

The story of Jesus' death and resurrection started to unfold on the previous evening, at the Last Supper. This marked the end of a ministry that had begun with turning water into wine at a wedding feast. It would end with symbolically turning wine into blood at a Jewish Passover feast.

Traditionally, four cups of wine are drunk. According to the sages, each is laden with meaning. The first cup remembers God saying, "I will take you out." The second, His promise: "I will save you." The third, another promise: "I will redeem you." And the fourth, yet another: "I will take you as a nation." Over the first cup, we say

Kiddush, the blessing for wine. Over the second, we tell the Exodus story. Over the third cup, we say grace after the meal. And over the fourth, we sing the Hallel.

Although things may have been done a little differently in Jesus' time, Jews today can identify with quite a lot of what the gospels tell us went on.

"While they were eating, Jesus took bread, and when He had given thanks, He broke it and gave it to his disciples, saying, 'Take and eat; this is my body'" (Matthew 26:26).

During the Seder, a piece of unleavened bread called the *afikomen*, Greek for "that which comes after," is broken and hidden. The children go in search of it and whoever finds it receives a reward. The bread Jesus broke, His "body given for you" (Luke 22:19), could have been the afikomen.

"Then He took a cup, and when He had given thanks, He gave it to them, saying, 'Drink from it, all of you. This is my blood of the covenant, which is poured out for many for the forgiveness of sins. I tell you, I will not drink from this fruit of the vine from now on until that day when I drink it new with you in my Father's kingdom'" (Matthew 26:27-29).

This would have been the third cup, the cup of redemption. Jesus took a vow at this time not to drink wine again until all that must be done had been completed. After His resurrection, He promised He would drink the fourth cup with His followers and take them as a nation.

"When they had sung a hymn, they went out to the Mount of Olives" (Matthew 26:30). The hymn they sang was very likely the Hallel. Since this accompanies the fourth cup, perhaps the disciples went ahead and drank theirs.

Butch and I made our first Passover Seder in Israel in Haifa. I was used to big, family Seders, but this was just the two of us. We ate our *matzot* crackers in the little kitchen of the apartment we were renting with a believer *haggadah,* the text that is read and recited at the Seder. It interwove Moses' and Jesus' Passover stories.

No bread or food containing leaven is eaten during the week-long festival. This is to remind us that the children of Israel left Egypt in haste, with no time to wait for their bread to rise. A rabbi in England once told me the setting aside of leaven actually originated in the annual cleaning of bread ovens. During this time only flatbread could be made. Hers was a practical explanation but something of a spoiler, I thought.

What constitutes leaven is not universally agreed upon among Jews. I ate rice. Many don't. I also ate chickpeas. Many Jews don't eat these either. Chickpeas in Hebrew is *hummus*, a word that, for some, may too closely resemble *chametz*, which means, "leaven." Avoiding these foods is based on tradition; there is no raising agent in either.

We moved on from the Garden Tomb to walk the ramparts of the Old City. The high fortress walls were built by the Turks in the 1600s. On the hillside opposite us was the Mount of Olives, where Jesus is expected to return. "On that day His feet will stand on the Mount of Olives, east of Jerusalem, and the Mount of Olives will be split in two from east to west, forming a great valley, with half of the mountain moving north and half moving south" (Zechariah 14:4).

The "man" who gave Ezekiel a vision of a future temple brought him to "the gate facing east, and I saw the glory of the God of Israel coming from the east. His voice was like the roar of rushing waters, and the land was radiant with his glory" (Ezekiel 43:1-2). The glory filled the temple. "I heard someone speaking to me from inside the temple. He said: 'Son of man, this is the place of my throne and the place for the soles of my feet. This is where I will live among the Israelites forever'" (vv. 6-7).

Looking back at Jerusalem from the Mount of Olives in the time of Jesus, the city would have been a spectacular sight. Anyone struggling up the steep slope from Jericho and rounding the mountain summit would be awed by their first glimpse of its white stone, nestling among sage-covered hills that stretched into infinity, exactly as it looks today, though its size has mushroomed.

Two arched bridges crossed the deep ravine ahead of Zion, the Upper City, with its marble villas and palaces. Below, by contrast, were the poorer, camel-colored limestone houses of the Lower City set on narrow, unpaved streets that sloped downhill and out of sight.

Perched high above the City of David was the greatest treasure of all and the most holy place in the Jewish world, the temple. Gleaming gold at the top of a steep, rocky slope, it was set on a large white stone platform that sloped down toward the eastern part of the city, with the effect that it appeared to tilt toward the Mount of Olives as if being presented on a tray. The temple proper, in the middle, was higher than the royal cloister and the outer walls, making it visible for many miles. Impressive doors, with lintels across the top of them, were as high as the great walls and adorned with veils embroidered with purple flowers. Between were pillars linked on high to one another by twisting vines of gold. What I wouldn't give to go back and sit at Jesus' feet as He taught in the temple courts!

The temple was God's dwelling place on earth. It is hardly surprising that Jesus should go to Gethsemane, at the base of the Mount of Olives, in full sight of His Father's house (Luke 2:49), on the most terrifying night of His life.

The name Gethsemane comes from *Gan Shemen*, "Oil Garden." There would once have been an oil press here. The arrest of Jesus in an oil garden is laden with symbolism. Oil presses had a link to the anointing of kings because the first and finest oil they produced, that which was allowed to drip down rather than pressed out of the olive, was set aside for anointing. The Hebrew word for Messiah, *Mashiach,* means "anointed one." An oil garden was a most appropriate place to begin the process that would consummate His kingship.

Leaving the disciples on watch, He went apart

LOVE TRIANGLES

from them to pray. Before them, blazing torches lit the temple. Above, the stars in the heavens burned brightly. The earth was a beautiful place and Jesus loved life. He threw himself down and prayed ardently that He might be given a little more time or, better still, be spared the horrific death He knew was coming.

"'Abba Father,' He said, 'everything is possible for you. Take this cup from me. Yet not what I will, but what you will'" (Mark 14:36).

Two thousand years before, God had spared His ancestor Abraham's only son on the site where the temple now stood. He would not be so lenient with His own.

An angel from heaven appeared to Jesus and strengthened Him as He prayed in an anguish such that sweat like drops of blood dripped to the ground. He stumbled to His feet, shivering a little in the cool spring night breeze. He hugged his robe to His body, the one the Roman soldiers would cast lots for the next day, the one woven of a single piece of cloth like the fine garments stipulated for the High Priest.

His disciples, made weary by the wine and song of the evening, combined with what may have been the intense spiritual oppression of the moment, let Him down. Instead of keeping watch as He had asked, He found them asleep, with no idea of what was about to happen, though He had told them again and again.

The hour for His arrest had come.

Feeling subdued, Butch and I wandered

through the Cardo, a restored Roman shopping mall with columns and other classical architectural features. We were on our way to the Western Wall, all that remains of the temple today.

After going through security, we found ourselves in the vast Western Wall Plaza. Ancient stones towered above us. A million scribbled prayers stuffed into the cracks fluttered like a flock of birds about to take flight. This was not my first visit. I had laid my hand on the Wall and felt electricity, the throb of thousands upon thousands of ardent petitions. But not today. Today I was thinking about what Jesus did, almost in this very spot, at Passover.

Surprisingly, what He did was clean His Father's house, like a Jewish housewife who diligently cleans and scrubs her home, removing from it every contaminating speck of leaven. Jesus cleansed His home of corruption. There was a half shekel temple tax that every Jew had to pay in temple currency. Only the temple moneychangers could transact the exchange and they were cheating their customers with unfair rates. Those selling doves for the most humble sacrifices were overcharging too. Enraged, Jesus made a whip of cords, overturned tables and benches, and drove out those who were buying and selling.

"It is written," He said, "'My house will be called a house of prayer,' but you are making it 'a den of robbers'" (Matthew 21:12-13).

He showed everyone what He meant by "a house of prayer" on the last and greatest day of the feast of Sukkot, when Jews dwell in shelters for a week, something it is actually warm enough for them to do in the fall in Israel. Sukkot was a time of joy, spent thanking God for his provision, as well as of supplication, offering requests for abundant rain to water the crops in the coming year.

It was *Hoshana Rabba*, the last and greatest day of the festival, marked by the great water-drawing ceremony. "Anyone who has not seen this water ceremony has never seen rejoicing in his life," an ancient rabbi wrote.

To the music of flutes, the High Priest led the faithful to the Pool of Siloam. He had a golden pitcher of wine and filled a second from the spring-fed "living waters" of the pool as the choir sang Psalm 118: "Give thanks to the Lord for He is good. His love endures forever," (v. 1) and the timely words, "Blessed is He who comes in the name of the Lord. From the House of the Lord we bless you" (v. 26).

In the silence that followed the blowing of the ram's horn shofar to announce the return, through the Water Gate, to the temple's great altar, where the water was poured out, Jesus stood and, in a loud voice, invited the throngs of pilgrims who had converged on the city to believe in Him and never thirst again (John 7:37-38).

He also told them, "I am the light of the world. Whoever follows me will never walk in darkness, but will have the light of life" (John 8:12). At Sukkot the temple was filled with enough light, it was said, to illuminate all the houses of Jerusalem.

Four hundred lamps blazed from high columns in the Courtyard of the Women while the men danced, wielding torches to underscore the festival's message that God was the Giver of Light.

I have made so very many connections between Jesus and His Jewish practice, traditions, and Scripture that I have wondered why the gospels do not mention what He did on the greatest Jewish festival of all, the Sabbath of Sabbaths and most holy day of the year, *Yom Kippur*. I have come to the conclusion that He joined Yom Kippur to Passover, rolling the two biggest festivals into one, through His death on the cross.

My friend Tom, whose story appears earlier in this book, points out that Passover is a festival connecting God to each family in Israel, whereas, Yom Kippur is "an interaction between God and Israel as a nation." He believes the two festivals will combine when all Israel enters into the New Covenant as a nation in fulfilment of Zechariah's prophecy: "On that day a fountain will be opened to the house of David and the inhabitants of Jerusalem, to cleanse them from sin and impurity" (Zechariah 13:1).

Today Israel is silent on Yom Kippur. Nothing is open and no one travels. If it weren't for the kids playing soccer in the middle of the highway, you might think everyone had left. Everyone is making atonement, even those who don't believe in God.

In my UK synagogue, we would confess our shortcomings, corporately and individually:

LOVE TRIANGLES

We have abused and betrayed. We are cruel.
We have destroyed and embittered other people's lives.
We were false to ourselves.
We have gossiped about others and hated them.
We have insulted and jeered. We have killed. We have lied.
We have misled others.
(From a traditional Jewish Prayer of Atonement)

Throughout the High Holy Days, which include Yom Kippur, we prayed to be written in the Book of Life for a good year. On Yom Kippur, this book was closed and our fates sealed for the year ahead. Jesus had no need of such prayers. He knew what lay ahead.

He had no shortcomings and no need to make confession. Yet He who came to fulfil, not overturn, the Law would have been obedient to Leviticus. He would have gone to the temple to afflict His soul by making the required twenty-five-hour fast, during which not even water is consumed.

The gospel writers don't ram home to us that Jesus, through His sacrifice at *Pesach*, became our Paschal Lamb. They just tell the story and expect us to get it. Perhaps Jesus' link to Yom Kippur was equally obvious to them.

His taking on our sins on the cross and atoning for us all reminds me strongly of the Yom Kippur ritual of the two goats that is still practiced by some Jews today. In the eastern part of the temple court, north of the great altar where sacrifices took place, two kid goats were brought for a sin offering. One would be designated for the Lord and the other, a scapegoat, taken to Azazel. This was a rocky clifftop in the Judean desert from which it would fall to its death.

The High Priest alone carried out all of the sacred tasks that had to be performed on Yom Kippur. Before the goat was sent out, the priest would make confession for the whole nation over the scapegoat's head. Aaron, the first High Priest, who lived in the time of Moses, was instructed how. "He is to lay both hands on the head of the live goat and confess over it all the wickedness and rebellion of the Israelites—all their sins—and put them on the goat's head. He shall send the goat away into the wilderness in the care of someone appointed for the task. The goat will carry on itself all their sins to a remote place; and the man shall release it in the wilderness" (Leviticus 16:21-22).

The High Priest designated Jesus as scapegoat for the sins of the whole Jewish nation. "Then one of them, named Caiaphas, who was High Priest that year, spoke up, 'You know nothing at all! You do not realize that it is better for you that one man die for the people than that the whole nation perish.' He did not say this on his own, but as High Priest that year he prophesied that Jesus would die for the Jewish nation, and not only for that nation but also for the scattered children of God, to bring them together and make them one. So from that day on they plotted to take his life" (John 11:49-

53). I have to wonder whether "that day" was Yom Kippur.

According to Revelation 20: 1-3, those sins will not remain forever on Jesus. They will ultimately be placed upon, "the serpent of old, who is the devil and Satan." "An angel coming down from heaven, holding the key of the abyss and a great chain in his hand" will throw Satan "into the abyss, and shut it and [seal] it over him, so that he [will] not deceive the nations any longer."

From my perspective, since Jesus became our atoning sacrifice, both the scapegoat that carried the sins away and the goat that was sacrificed for the Lord, at Passover, I no longer needed to pray at Yom Kippur to be written in the Book of Life. He has done that for me.

Jesus' death on the cross gave us immediate and direct access to God. This happened when the curtain to the Holy of Holies was ripped in two as He died. Formerly, the High Priest alone could come into God's presence, and that only on Yom Kippur. "No one is to be in the tent of meeting from the time Aaron goes in to make atonement in the Most Holy Place until he comes out, having made atonement for himself, his household and the whole community of Israel" (Leviticus 16:17). He did this wearing white linen clothes that he would never put on again. They would be left in the place where he removed them.

Jesus entered the tomb alone, just as the High Priest entered the Holy of Holies, wrapped in white linen that He would never wear again. That was on

Friday evening, as Sabbath, the day of rest, and Pesach, the festival of freedom, came in, together. Three days later, a new world began as He rose from the dead. Sunday in Hebrew is *yom rishon* or "first day," set aside to remember God's creation.

Mary Magdalene found the tomb empty. She ran to tell the others, who were sitting *shiva*, the seven days of housebound mourning observant Jews carry out.

"So Peter and the other disciple started for the tomb. Both were running, but the other disciple outran Peter and reached the tomb first. He bent over and looked in at the strips of linen lying there but did not go in. Then Simon Peter came along behind him and went straight into the tomb. He saw the strips of linen lying there, as well as the cloth that had been wrapped around Jesus' head. The cloth was still lying in its place, separate from the linen" (John 20:3-7).

The white linen was important enough to be mentioned three times. The gospel writer was making the point, as the writer of Hebrews would, that through the cross, Jesus became our eternal High Priest.

What began at the crucifixion was completed at Pentecost, the Jewish festival of Shavuot. What better season for Jesus to ascend to heaven and send down His Holy Spirit, the Helper He had promised, than that which commemorated Moses' descent from the mountain, struggling under the weight of God's Law engraved on tablets of stone? Weighing nothing at all, the Holy Spirit would enter our hearts, guide our conscience, and support our faith in God's loving protection.

The disciples were gathered together in one place, most likely in the temple courts close to where Butch and I now stood. The Holy Spirit descended in a rushing wind and tongues of flame. Led by Peter, they all begin to evangelize the startled crowd that had gathered, pilgrims for Shavuot from many different countries, like the crowd all around Butch and me. The disciples spoke to them with power and authority about Jesus. Those who heard were also filled with the Holy Spirit.

Even non-Jews could receive the Spirit, as Peter would later discover to his amazement when he evangelized a Roman centurion and his household.

Jesus had left His disciples with the instruction to witness for Him everywhere and make disciples of all nations. Right here, under a heavenly blue sky, a bright sun shining on the white stone walls of Jerusalem, was where they began doing that. Some 3,000 were brought to faith that day.

I too was brought to faith here in Jerusalem and for that I am immeasurably grateful. "I will praise the LORD all my life; I will sing praise to my God as long as I live" (Psalm 146:2).

Chapter 7 — Doing Church Israeli Style

"For He Himself is our peace, who has made the two groups one and has destroyed the barrier, the dividing wall of hostility, by setting aside in His flesh the Law with its commands and regulations. His purpose was to create in Himself one new humanity out of the two, thus making peace, and in one body to reconcile both of them to God through the cross, by which He put to death their hostility" (Ephesians 2:14-16).

On our first Friday evening as volunteers in Israel, the worship band at Beit Immanuel sang with gusto to welcome in the Sabbath:
Rak ata Raoui (boom, boom)
Rak ata Raoui (boom, boom)
Rak ata Raoui le t'filotai
(boom, boom, boom, boom)
The lyrics translated, "Only You are worthy (x3) of my prayer."
The music was neither rock praise, in the North American style, nor lyrical, like many British worship songs. It was more, well, euro-pop, catchy

LOVE TRIANGLES

and memorable. If it hadn't been in Hebrew, I would probably have gone around singing the words instead of humming them. Back then I hadn't yet got my head around the *aleph-bet*. Luckily there was transliteration on the screen at the front for me to try and sound out.

In time I would understand that the way the praise band belted out the songs was a major trump card of this congregation and thus, a kind of outreach that drew in Russian families. Almost the whole congregation was Russian.

After the singing we donned headsets to hear simultaneous translation. The minister, an American, preached and prayed in Hebrew as did his assistant, a Russian. The Sunday school teacher, also a Russian, gave out notices in Hebrew, although today wasn't Sunday but Friday and most of the parents would have preferred to hear them in Russian.

As the weeks went by, we would discover that the translation coming into our ears could range from good to incomprehensible to mostly silent, depending on who was feeding us English, invariably not their mother tongue.

Fast forward about seven months to the late spring of 2010. By then, having completed our Aliyah, we were settled as citizens in Haifa. I was well into my Ulpan course in Hebrew and doing a lot better with worship in Israel.

Butch had started working for the *Or haCarmel* Congregation at the top of Mount Carmel. He could have done Ulpan with me. Indeed, that was our original plan and he made a start. Unlike me, however, he had never tackled a foreign language and got hung up on learning his aleph-bet, which wasn't how he learned English as a baby. It was too hard; so he dropped out.

His job at Or haCarmel was maintenance. He worked through the summer on the roof of the magnificent congregation building, installing air conditioning. The work was physical and it was hot. He would come home, shower, and climb into bed for a couple of hours.

After Ulpan I joined the staff to work on events. I loved starting each workday with praise and prayer. It helped me focus on keeping the right attitude at work, which was not always easy. We were all imperfect human beings trying to do God's will as perfectly as we were able. I was not sure, at first, I was in the right place. Then, one morning, God showed me that I was exactly where He intended me to be.

I was searching through my computer files for a map my boss wanted when I was shocked to come across a photograph of myself wearing my tallit, the beautiful handmade prayer shawl I'd had designed to celebrate my adult Bat Mitzvah in the UK about eight years before. The picture was taken from a Jewish magazine that had run an article about it.

Part of a *Guide to Jewish Practices* for a previous school of ministry handout, the picture had been downloaded in September, 2007 by a predecessor. A Google search for "prayer shawl" yielded 576,000 responses. The odds that an old picture of me should happen to be downloaded to a computer in Israel on which I would later work had to be infinitesimal. In September 2007 I knew nothing about Or haCarmel and Or haCarmel had most certainly never heard of me. At that time, I was on my first visit to Eastern Canada, following signs and wonders that would lead me to meet and marry Butch.

I took this as God telling me I was to stay.

The programs I worked on included communicating the nearness of end times, for which the return of the Jews was a marker, to visitors from all over the world. In his book *God's Tsunami*, Peter Tsukahira, school of ministry founder and leader, argues that the wave of sharing the message of Christ has been moving relentlessly westward since Jesus initially preached it in Israel.

The apostle Paul took it to Europe where, over hundreds of years, it spread across the continent, jumping across the Atlantic Ocean at the end of the Middle Ages to the newly discovered Americas. It continued westward with the settlers. It is currently creating a furor in the Far East, where congregations numbering 30,000 or more are not uncommon. And it continues towards India and the Middle East. Peter believes that when the message has come full circle, back to the Jews of Israel, the end will come.

Our Messianic congregation was not popular with the Israeli authorities and our leaders had been blacklisted. Why did it have to be this way? We could hardly be categorized as that dreaded word in Israel, "missionaries." Our outreach was primarily to existing Christians, inciting them to value Israel. Our efforts toward the local Israeli population were low-key and minimal. On Monday evenings through the summer, we would go down to the beach, where we sang songs, handed out tracts, and talked to anyone who wanted to know more. I say *we*, but I was careful not to do more than pray for those having the conversations. I didn't want to risk being seen and getting myself blacklisted.

The authorities have been known to rescind the rights of olim who follow Jesus. As a citizen I could fight such a move in the courts. But if I was that unwelcome, would I really want to force the issue?

Other congregations in Israel can be equally restrained in their outreach. Immanuel Church, the beautiful Lutheran church in Jaffa, just across from Beit Immanuel, was that way. Older than the whole neighboring city of Tel Aviv, it was seen as historic. Its lovely stained glass windows depicting Peter raising Tabitha from the dead and Jonah taking a ship from Jaffa attracted many visitors. Organ recitals were held to packed audiences.

The local cosmopolitan Jewish population seemed less afraid than they might once have been of stepping over the threshold of a church. This may have arisen from the self-assurance that comes from living in a Jewish state. Or maybe it was indicative of growing secularity among Jews living in the Land. Either way, Immanuel Church was careful not to step on toes. It pulled the people in but did not push the faith.

Pastor Christian, the Danish minister, and I made contact with the Alpha Course leadership at HTB, Holy Trinity Brompton Church, in London, my former home church in the UK, with a view to bringing it to Israel. The course, run by churches throughout the world, explains the Christian faith to anyone interested in learning more about it.

Bringing the course to Israel was already on HTB's agenda, we discovered. Christian and I were in agreement, however, that in order to serve Jews, it would need tweaking. HTB didn't seem to understand the need for this. Neither did Butch when I shared our feelings with him. He was outraged. "What's so special about the Jews that they need to hear the message in a special way?" he asked.

I think he thought we were suggesting it should be diluted for them. That wasn't it. It was obvious to Christian and me that the Jews already had a perfectly good God, the same one as the Christians, and a perfectly good book, the Tanach. They even believed in the Messiah. In fact the idea of Him was originally given to the Jews by God.

What they refuted was that the Messiah was Jesus. Their need was not so much for the arguments of historicity the Alpha course offered as for proofs that the Tanach pointed towards Him. That was the strategy of the early Jewish believers in Acts.

It may surprise some Christians who skim through Matthew 1, the genealogy of Christ, to learn that this is one of the most powerful passages in the New Testament for Jewish seekers. It demonstrates Jesus' legitimacy in the Jewish continuum from Patriarch Abraham down through David, the beloved king.

Many aspects of the Alpha Course would be relevant to Jews on the verge of accepting Him, not least its focus on the Holy Spirit. In the end Christian did run it at Immanuel Church. It was announced in the church newsletter but was not otherwise publicized. It served to explain the foundations of the Christian faith to the church's existing members and was well-attended by them.

Beit Eliyahu, the Lutheran-supported Messianic congregation in downtown Haifa, a five-minute walk from where we lived, were our landlords. We joined an English language home group there, run by Sam, an American. It was attended by a mix of local residents and volunteers at the congregation's nursing home for the elderly, some of whom were Holocaust survivors. There were Scandinavians, Russians, Americans, Germans, Australians, Mexicans, and Israelis.

We all got along very well. The only time we argued was when some Jewish members said that, since they were the Chosen People of God, they were preferred. This did not go over well with the Gentiles present or, for that matter, with Sam, a Jew, or myself.

LOVE TRIANGLES

We also enjoyed Beit Eliyahu's monthly Friday night Shabbat suppers, where candles were lit and songs sung.

Although we usually drove up the mountain to worship at Or haCarmel, we liked the worship at Beit Eliyahu very much. It was a much smaller congregation than Or haCarmel and very friendly. Pastor Shmuel Aweida delivered sermons in simple Hebrew that even I could understand. His outreach strategy was to encourage us to share our personal testimonies with others. I attended a short course on weeknights to practice doing this in small groups.

There was something special about Shmuel, a gentle and caring Arab man married to a Norwegian wife. When babies were born, you would find Shmuel visiting the new parents at the hospital. When a fourteen-year-old girl from his congregation got blown up on the bus coming home from school, he buried her.

Abigail Little was coming home on the public bus one ordinary weekday in March 2003 when, just one stop from her home, the suicide bomber standing beside her detonated the explosives strapped to his body under his clothing. The bus, packed with students, exploded and metal shrapnel inside the bomb flew in all directions, causing horrific injuries. Abigail died instantly, along with sixteen others. A further fifty-three people were injured. Pastor Shmuel was the first at the hospital. He identified Abigail's body and broke the terrible news to Phil and Heidi Litle, her parents.

More than 1,000 mourners, Messianic believers and non-believers, neighbors and school friends, attended her funeral. Phil and Heidi are Americans. The US Ambassador attended as well as an Israeli government representative and the mayor of Haifa. National and international media covered the funeral.

Standing beside Abigail's casket, draped with Israeli and American flags, Phil spoke of dreams for his daughter's future that would never be fulfilled and about the void her death had left in the hearts of her family. He went on to confess his confidence that Abigail was fully alive in heaven with Yeshua, her Savior. They would all surely meet again face to face and forever.

Pastor Shmuel and Abigail's friends spoke of the impact her faith and love had had on those around her. As they spoke, sunshine broke through the clouds and flooded the cemetery. A TV correspondent, hardened by the many such funerals she had covered, was brought to tears. The police commander in charge of security at the funeral, a firm unbeliever, acknowledged the "truth" of the Messianic faith, as did the Israeli government representative with whom Pastor Shmuel had shared the gospel the previous day. After the funeral Shmuel continued to share the Messianic message in interviews for radio and television in Hebrew and English.

As we interacted with the people at Beit Eliyahu through 2010 and 2011, we were unaware, at first, that Phil, the American who welcomed us with a firm handshake and a smile at the door, was Abigail's father or that Heidi, the friendly American lady I sometimes chatted with, was her mother. We did not know, either, that Josiah, who often translated Shmuel's message through our headsets, was her brother or that the elderly couple from Missouri attending our home group through the summer were her grandparents.

Their strength has made a lasting impression on us. How deep is the love of the Litle family for Israel that they should bury their American daughter in the Land and that they should stay when they might have fled and that Josiah should choose to serve in the IDF when he didn't have to.

Their permanent residency is a right accorded by Israel to victims of terrorism. They view their commitment to Israel as permanent. Phil, formerly the head of the Baptist Convention in Israel and now national director of *Or b'Aretz*, "Light of the Land," an affiliate of Campus Crusade for Christ, says of their decision to stay, "It is very difficult to understand danger when you only hear about it. But if you believe in Israel like we do and you believe that God is at work here, then you have to ask yourself the question 'Do I believe in it enough that it could cost me personally?'"

That is a question Jews who choose to live in Israel also have to ask themselves. Many have had cause to tremble in fear for their lives as they have scrambled to don gas masks and put them on their children. Many like our friends Zafrir and Aviva in Chapter 1 have had missiles fired at them or have had to flee their homes.

Pastor Dani Sayag, one of the leaders at Or haCarmel, wrote a favorite Hebrew worship song of mine, *Chaim Lanetzach*, in memory of Abigail. The title means "Eternal Life." Pastor Dani, a Jewish Israeli, is good friends with Pastor Shmuel, an Arab Israeli leading a Jewish Messianic congregation. The suicide bomber, a twenty-year-old Hamas member, was also an Arab Israeli, as was the Arab resident of Haifa who planned the attack and who is now serving a life sentence.

Arab Israelis were our neighbors in Haifa. We lived in a Christian Arab area. A few of our neighbors were Moslem. The Dell repair guy who fixed my laptop pulled a face and asked me what I was doing living in such an area. He thought I was crazy, but they were good people, all of them. They got on well with each other and with us, although my putting up a *mezuzah* at our front door may have been one step too far for them. It disappeared within the day.

Haifa is known for its religious tolerance. When Butch had a biopsy on his leg, which, thank the Lord, would turn out to be nothing sinister, the Arab nurse and *Ashkenazi* Jewish doctor performing the procedure chatted away like best friends throughout the operation.

Israeli Arabs and Jews have identical rights, healthcare, and study opportunities in Israel. Even so, my neighbors grumbled about the regime. Though they were not second class citizens, they always seemed to feel like they were.

LOVE TRIANGLES

Or haCarmel countered the prejudice and resentment on both sides through a vision that centered on the concept of One New Man, as described in Ephesians 2:14-16: "For He Himself is our peace, who has made the two groups one, (Jew and Gentile), and has destroyed the barrier, the dividing wall of hostility, by setting aside in His flesh the Law with its commands and regulations. His purpose was to create in Himself one new humanity out of the two, thus making peace, and in one body to reconcile both of them to God through the cross, by which He put to death their hostility."

Our leaders preached and lived out a unity between Jew, Arab, and Gentile. Leaders David Davis and Peter Tsukahira are Gentiles. Pastor Dani Sayag is Jewish, as is Karen Davis, David's American-born wife, who leads the worship team. Pastor Vladimir Tsapar is a Russian Jew. Two larger-than-life Arab personalities with their own congregations are also on board.

Joseph Haddad was our lively simultaneous interpreter of sermons. He turned David Davis and Peter Tsukahira's English into Hebrew, as well as Dani Sayag's Hebrew into English, for us. He did a great job. If the preacher got worked up, he got worked up. If he took a step forward or back, Joseph stepped with him.

Joseph is a Christian Arab of Lebanese descent. He found his true vocation when 6,000 Lebanese refugees poured into Israel in May 2,000. They were sent to a kibbutz near the border. The next day, Joseph and David Davis went to help them. "We filled two vans with diapers and baby food, powdered milk and Arab Bibles, and we drove up to the kibbutz," Joseph said.

Seeing the desperation and bewilderment of the refugees, Joseph's wife set up her keyboard and they began singing worship songs. A crowd gathered to hear David Davis' message. It was based on Isaiah 29:17-21: "In a very short time, will not Lebanon be turned into a fertile field and the fertile field seem like a forest? In that day the deaf will hear the words of the scroll, and out of gloom and darkness the eyes of the blind will see. Once more the humble will rejoice in the Lord; the needy will rejoice in the Holy One of Israel. The ruthless will vanish, the mockers will disappear, and all who have an eye for evil will be cut down—those who with a word make someone out to be guilty, who ensnare the defender in court and with false testimony deprive the innocent of justice."

Joseph, who was translating into Arabic, saw that those who heard the message "were amazed to hear that Lebanon was mentioned in the Bible and it was such a blessing for them to hear David preaching about their homeland in this way."

Joseph first met David Davis when he came to work at the House of Victory, the addiction center David and Karen founded when they first came to Israel in 1989. They have achieved outstanding successes. Israeli social workers who have wanted to know their secret have been reluctant to believe that the Bible is the only rehabilitation tool used.

LOVE TRIANGLES

David and Karen's Or haCarmel congregation has grown exponentially. In the early 1990s they built the beautiful kehilah congregation building with the welcome addition, in 2010, of the air conditioning Butch and others worked on through the summer. As well as the school of ministry and annual convocation events that I helped organize, Peter Tsukahira's wife, Rita, has founded a thriving home for refugee women and their children, escapees to Israel from politically difficult countries like Sudan.

Joseph grew up not liking Jews at all. Media, newspapers, and talk on the street filled his head with the idea that the Jews were oppressing the Arabs, whose land they had taken. All that changed after he accepted Jesus as his Savior in 1984. His turning point came while reading Joel 3:2: "I will gather all nations and bring them down to the Valley of Jehoshaphat. There I will put them on trial for what they did to my inheritance, my people Israel, because they scattered my people among the nations and divided up my land."

He realized, "If it is God's land and He gave it to the Jews, who am I to resist Him or oppose Him?"

Joseph now has his own Arab-speaking congregation in Nahariya. Many members are the refugees he and David ministered to back in 2,000. Recently, however, something else has started happening, something amazing: Jewish people are starting to come to the meetings.

The Lebanese are reaching out to their Jewish

neighbors and bringing them into his congregation. As they come to faith, Arab Pastor Joseph is baptizing them. Maybe, one day, Zafrir and Aviva, my lovely friends from Nahariya, will join them.

The second Arab you will find on the podium during Saturday morning worship at Or haCarmel is Yousef Dakwar, who plays a mean electric guitar with the worship team. Like Joseph, Yousef was born in Haifa and went to Catholic school there. His family was from Berram, a small village whose name means "fruitful," situated just on the Israeli side of the Lebanese border. He was raised with a deep hatred towards Israel and the Jewish people.

In 1948 the newly-created State of Israel was forced to defend every one of its borders, including that with Lebanon. Some IDF soldiers came and ordered the evacuation of Berram. The residents were fearful. They had heard stories from the Galilee area about Jews destroying Arab villages to eliminate snipers. Rather than move away, they went to live in caves nearby. It was November and they were cold. Soon they were hungry too—and sick from drinking dirty water. Seven of their children died from the harsh conditions.

The Israeli Minister for Minorities called a meeting in their village, to which the village priest also came. They explained that it was necessary to evacuate the village for about two weeks for the villagers' own protection. Leaving everything behind in their houses and taking only their livestock with them, the villagers stayed with neighbors in a nearby village.

LOVE TRIANGLES

They never did return. Berram was razed to the ground by the IDF. As a boy, Yousef's father would take him there. They would sit on the scattered stones that were once the walls of the family home and his father would weep. Unsurprisingly, Yousef became angry and resentful.

After he was claimed by Jesus at a youth conference, it was his turn to weep. The verses about One New Man from Ephesians 2 were key to his complete change of heart.

"I prayed and asked the Lord to put to death the enmity that was living in me," he said. "After that, everything changed in my life and I started to pray for the salvation of the Jewish people. I forgave everything they had done to me and, along with my wife, eventually became part of a Messianic Jewish congregation."

Yousef's vision is of the "highway from Egypt to Assyria," prophesied in Isaiah 19:22. He sees all worshiping together. "In that day, Israel will be the third, along with Egypt and Assyria, a blessing on the earth. The Lord Almighty will bless them, saying, 'Blessed be Egypt my people, Assyria my handiwork, and Israel my inheritance'" (Isaiah 19:24-25).

I have heard David Davis preach vigorously on the oft-repeated biblical phrase "in that day." He believes "that day" is already dawning.

American Tom Hess, founder of the Jerusalem House of Prayer for all Nations, has done much towards making Isaiah 19 a reality, not only through a constant prayer vigil in Jerusalem but also through the organization of convocations, bringing Arab Christian leaders from all over the Middle East together with Messianic leaders from Israel to forge friendship and understanding in the Ephesians 2 spirit.

Yousef has his own Arab congregation that meets in a former cinema in downtown Haifa. Media-trained in Canada, he is using broadcasting to bring the gospel to the Middle East through an internet radio station he founded, *Radio Atareeq*, which means "The Way." He jokes that, at first, his mother and his wife were his only listeners. Now he is getting millions of hits every month. The popularity of his station is helping complete the wave of faith heading relentlessly westward that Peter Tsukahira has identified in *God's Tsunami*.

Love of Jesus is breaking down barriers and clearing a path for Arabs to love Jews and Jews to love Arabs. Those who have fixed their eyes on God to seek to know and do His will, rather than follow their own agendas, have found hope for peace born of refined hearts.

When this unifying love is absent, what you can get is the difficult kind of standoff that has marred the budding friendship between Mike, our Jewish believer friend from the USA in Chapter 5, and Abud.

Mike met Abud while volunteering in Nazareth and they quickly became friends. One evening, as they were eating dinner together, Abud threw into the conversation the question "Why don't they give back the land?"

LOVE TRIANGLES

He was talking about the Golan Heights, a part of Israel that was formerly Syrian. Butch and I took a short vacation in this beautiful area in 2011. The berry orchards of the kibbutz where we stayed were just a couple hundred yards from the wire border fence. White UN Jeeps patrolled up and down in front of it and a large Syrian flag waved on the opposite side as we picked our fruit, keeping a wary eye.

Mike's answer to Abud was that the missiles being fired on Israel out of Gaza made any discussion of a return of the Golan impossible. Abud did not agree.

In the end Mike said, "Abud, politics is a topic I don't think we can talk about. If we do, then I don't think we can be friends."

They have never since discussed any kind of sensitive issue. Mike and Abud cannot be real with one another, a challenge I understand well, since I have had such difficulty being open about my faith in Jesus around my fellow Israelis. I would have loved to have felt free to discuss what I believed with those who needed to hear it.

George Woodward, formerly president of the 700 Club, Canada, and his wife, Marilyn, are helping Messianic congregations in Israel spread the word about Jesus through their organization, Israel's Peace Ministries. They believe the most effective way to get His message out to the Jews of Israel is to bring encouragement and real financial support to struggling and oppressed congregations in the Land. George discovered early on that about eighteen of the approximately 130 Messianic congregations in Israel are quite heavily persecuted.

His ministry had to be selective in order to be effective. "Currently, we have five congregations that we are supporting on a quite substantial financial basis every month," George told me.

The congregations are dotted around the country and a sixth is about to be added.

Israel's Peace Ministries' funding must be used for the furtherance of the gospel. In a climate where those who believe in Yeshua may be spoken to harshly, shunned, or even physically attacked, it is hard for me to imagine how persecuted Messianics might do more than say to outsiders, "We are here."

"They find very unique ways to evangelize," George explained, citing the example of a congregation that rented a tour bus to take new olim, predominantly Russians, around Israel, visiting and explaining all the Messianic Bible sites.

He also told me that, despite all the dangers, Messianic Jews, certain that God has called them to try and save their people, seemed prepared go out on the streets to evangelize. "The pastor in Ashdod and some of his young men are very bold," George said.

He believes there will come a time when Messianic Judaism will be tolerated legally. I certainly hope so, although lawyer Joshua Pex saw no sign of that happening in the foreseeable future.

I asked George where his love of Messianic

LOVE TRIANGLES

Jews in Israel sprang from. He told me about a television program he was watching some years back in which a Jew mentioned that Jewish followers of the Messiah in Israel were persecuted. The remark caught his attention.

"I couldn't get away from it. It sort of rang within me for a number of months, to the point where I had to find out if it was really true," George said. "And, of course, it is."

He looked for an organization he could support in overcoming this situation but was unable to find one. So he founded his own. When I asked him about the biggest hurdle his ministry faced, he bemoaned the "complacency and a sort of a ho-hum attitude about supporting Israel, even prayerfully, in a western setting. There is almost a 're-all-falling-asleep' attitude across the Christian church."

"What would you say to wake them up?" I asked.

"Read your Bible!" George retorted.

He would refer them, in particular, to the verse in Genesis 12 where God tells Abraham, "I will bless those who bless you, and whoever curses you I will curse; and all peoples on earth will be blessed through you."

"Jesus will return to the Mount of Olives, not to Everest or somewhere in the Rockies," George said. "We need to get on board, supporting God's people, as the Bible asks us to."

I thought how all the famous Jesus places were in Israel—Bethlehem where He was born,

Nazareth where He grew up, the Sea of Galilee where much of His ministry took place and Jerusalem where He was crucified and rose again. It was hard to understand how anyone could dismiss the siting of all those events as irrelevant.

Chapter 8 — Unto Us a Son is Given

"Joseph son of David, do not be afraid to take Mary home as your wife, because what is conceived in her is from the Holy Spirit. She will give birth to a Son, and you are to give Him the name Jesus, because He will save his people from their sins" (Matthew 1:20-21).

On Christmas Eve, 2009, all the volunteers at Beit Immanuel went to Bethlehem, except Butch and me.

They thought it was a special thing to do on the birthday of Jesus and expected it to be a special place. Some 700 years before His birth, the prophet Micah predicted, "But you, Bethlehem Ephrathah, though you are small among the clans of Judah, out of you will come for Me one who will be ruler over Israel, whose origins are from of old, from ancient times" (Micah 5:2).

Now that a wall separated Bethlehem from Jerusalem, I really didn't want to risk any kind of stamp on my passport, particularly one dated Christmas Eve. Such a blatantly Christian excursion would not help the application to make Aliyah we were seriously considering making.

Other reasons contributed to our decision not to go. People would be shoulder to shoulder in Bethlehem's little main square and I hated crowds like that. Also, the bus from Jerusalem could get into a lengthy line-up at the checkpoint, making the journeying time unpredictable.

I preferred to freeze-frame biblical Bethlehem in my mind's eye; the city of my imagining would be much more attractive than reality. Naomi, Ruth, her husband, Boaz, and David, the boy who would be king, would all be there, visiting Baby Jesus.

Bethlehem was Naomi's hometown to which she returned with her Moabite daughter-in-law, Ruth, after their menfolk died in Moab. My vision was of the two women arriving in late March or April at the end of the latter rains and the start of what would be bumper barley and wheat harvests.

Bethlehem, which means "House of Bread," was the breadbasket of Israel, renowned for its farming. Grain was not its only crop. Grapevines, olives, figs, and pomegranates were watered by springs, tunneled through rock to fertile terraces.

On the hillsides outside of town, shepherds guarded their sheep. David, Ruth's future great-grandson, minded his father's flock, filling the hours of solitude with slingshot practice. He thought he was training himself to protect the sheep in his charge from marauding animals like wolves and hyenas. In reality, God was training him to bring down the smug giant, Goliath, with a single stone.

Though this pastoral idyll of Bethlehem was great, the story of Jesus' birth there was even greater. "For to us a Child is born, to us a Son is given, and the government will be on His shoulders. And He will be called Wonderful Counselor, Mighty God, Everlasting Father, Prince of Peace. Of the greatness of his government and peace there will be no end" (Isaiah 9:6).

As Joseph fussed around the newborn, conscious of the huge responsibility he had been given in bringing up God's Son, Jesus' mother laid Him in a manger from which livestock would be fed because there was no room at the inn. The Greek word the Bible uses is *kataluma*, which means "guest room." It is the same word Mark 14:14-15 uses to describe the large, furnished upstairs room where the Last Supper took place.

It may well have been a room in the house of relatives that was not available to Mary and Joseph because it was already occupied by other family members. The mention of a manger does not necessarily mean they wound up outside. Houses where animals lived cheek to jowl with the family during the cooler months were commonplace. Their body heat helped humans keep warm and their dung served as a source of fuel.

The events leading up to Jesus' birth began in Nazareth, just up the road from our Haifa home. Nazareth was somewhere Butch and I would come to know well. With its hinged wooden door shopfronts and workshops, open markets and stalls selling Middle Eastern foods, in many ways, it still looked biblical. An unfortunate damper was a huge anti-Christian billboard erected by the Arab population that you could not fail to pass as you walked up the hill toward the Church of the Annunciation.

In spite of this turn-off, our first visit to the church, late in 2009, wound up feeling supernaturally wonderful. The Church of the Annunciation is a lovely place, beautified by decorated plaques from many nations and massive carved wooden doors.

On that day, it was crowded. Busloads of tourists were milling around, seemingly more interested in tourism than in Jesus. My view of my fellow pilgrims softened as we lined up behind some Greek women to see Mary's Cave. Their simple hymn-singing was a delight.

After this the afternoon was drawing to an end. The tourists headed back to their buses. Butch and I remained by the altar. I closed my eyes and prayed about our decision regarding Aliyah. Should we stay? When I opened my eyes and looked around, the church has empty, not one tourist, not one priest. We were alone in the huge, towering church. In awe we smiled at one another, taking the void as a blessing. Looking back, perhaps God was showing me a picture of the isolation I would feel. If so, I should have understood His message that there would be a peace in being true to myself.

Mary understood this immediately. As a young,

LOVE TRIANGLES

devout woman, her plans would not have involved a pregnancy ahead of her wedding night, but she willingly accepted what God asked of her, though it would see her judged, perhaps vilified.

The Nazareth part of Joseph and Mary's story started with a betrothal, a *mazal tov* for good luck and a *l'chaim*—"to life!"—as the couple toasted the seal on their marriage with a cup of wine. The two smiled shyly at one another as they sipped from the shared cup. The bride price Joseph would pay Mary's father had been agreed upon. The father and the groom each got a copy of the *ketubah*, the "marriage contract." A third was sealed and lodged with the synagogue. Joseph gave Mary a gift, a gold coin perhaps, as a token of his esteem.

The pair would see little of one another in the months that followed as Joseph built a bride room, possibly an addition to an existing three-generational family home, where the marriage would be consummated.

Although this was an arranged marriage, it promised to be a happy one. Both were strong in the faith. Miri, as Joseph called her—short for Miriam—was a good girl, not the sort to run around on him. Miri was content with her groom. A carpenter, he was not a wealthy man but a literate one, active in the synagogue, who would pass on his knowledge of the Scriptures to their children. Their combined Jewish pedigrees were illustrious, both being descendants of King David.

All was good in their lives until the day Mary came to Joseph's workshop, which was filled with the sickly scent of resin and the nutty odor of woodchips. He looked up from the plow he was repairing and smiled to see her

She told him she was pregnant. The child was not his. "I have not known a man," she said.

He turned away to hide the hurt. "Yeah, right."

He wondered how she could remain so calm. Didn't she know that everything was ruined? He should report her unfaithfulness, have her stoned. He clenched and unclenched his fists. Maybe that would wipe the saintly expression off her face.

He returned to his lathe work. "Who's the father?"

Her voice was filled with passion as she told him that the child was of the Holy Spirit. "The angel Gabriel called me highly favored and blessed among women."

He didn't buy it. "Nice for you."

"I was terrified," she said. "I didn't understand, not at first."

"So what did he look like, this Gabriel?"

"Like an angel."

His mind was racing. How would she know what an angel looked like? Angels came to Bible heroes. They didn't come to Nazareth.

"He told me I'd conceive a child and call him Yeshua because He will rescue. He will be great and reign over the House of Jacob forever."

"A bastard from Nazareth?" Joseph sneered. "Or are you hoping I'll give him a name?" Despite his rage, he was moved by the tears that welled in her eyes.

LOVE TRIANGLES

"I see you don't believe," she said. "I'm sorry for that. I don't have an explanation that you would understand of how all this could have happened."

"Really, Miri?" He wiped the sawdust from his hands on his leather apron. "Do you think I was born yesterday?"

"The angel said, 'With God nothing is impossible.'" She left, saying with quiet dignity, "The Lord has done great things for me. Future generations shall call me blessed."

As his anger burned in the days that followed, these words would chase around like bees inside his head. After three days, he sought her out at the well, where all the women giggled to see Miri's bridegroom. The light of the whole world was shining in her eyes. Her serenity was bewildering.

He fell into step beside her as she headed for home with a full jug upon her shoulder. "You should leave town, the farther away the better," he said. "Where can you go?"

She thought for a moment. "My cousin Elizabeth is expecting her first baby though she's old. I can go help her."

"Good." He fought off the lump that balled in his throat. "While you're gone, I'll draw up the divorce papers and present them to your father."

He stared straight ahead, aware that she had turned to look at him. "It will be done quietly," he promised.

"My father is expecting the marriage to proceed. He's convinced the child is yours, no matter what I say."

"I wish it were."

"You wouldn't say that if you understood."

He missed Miri when she was gone. He wondered, through the long days, how she was doing.

Some words from Isaiah kept haunting him: "Therefore the Lord himself will give you a sign: the virgin will conceive and give birth to a son, and will call him Immanuel" (Isaiah 7:14).

He was thinking he would go up to Jerusalem for Tabernacles. He might run into Miri there. Maybe he would find himself at Elizabeth and her husband, Zachariah's, door on the way. No, he told himself, sawing furiously at some planks. He should put all this behind him, get those divorce papers drawn up. What was he waiting for?

That night Joseph had the strangest dream. An angel appeared to him. Now he knew what an angel looked like.

"Do not be afraid to take Miri as your wife," the angel said.

"I'm not afraid!"

"The child she has conceived is of the Holy Spirit."

"I know," Joseph said. He was startled by his own words. Had he, then, believed her all along?

"Her child is a son. You shall call Him Yeshua because He will save His people from their sins."

Joseph awoke filled with a sense of the supernatural and feeling closer to God than ever before. He paced the roof under the bright stars,

LOVE TRIANGLES

unburdened of the stain of betrayal he had been carrying.

Instead, he was being honored by God with the greatest opportunity to serve Him any man had ever had. He felt the weight of responsibility for the Child that would be entrusted into his care and vowed to be the most devoted husband and father in the world.

Early the next morning, Joseph told Miri's father he was going to bring his wife home. He began to explain his dream, but the man did not need to hear his words.

"You are doing what is right," Miri's father said.

Joseph fetched Miri from helping her cousin with the birth of the boy who would grow up to be John the Baptist. He did not take her to his own house but to her father's, where she would remain, he thought, until the child's birth.

Their plans changed when "Caesar Augustus issued a decree that a census should be taken of the entire Roman world. (This was the first census that took place while Quirinius was governor of Syria.) And everyone went to their own town to register. So Joseph also went up from the town of Nazareth in Galilee to Judea, to Bethlehem the town of David, because he belonged to the house and line of David" (Luke 2:1-4).

Joseph's family, who were Judeans, had probably moved to the Galilee region a century before. Possibly Mary's family had done the same. Many archaeological finds confirm the presence of

Judeans working the rich agricultural land of the Galilee at this time. Judeans moved there, encouraged by King Alexander Janneaus of Judea who tried throughout his twenty-five year reign to repopulate the Galilean countryside that had lain desolate for some 600 years after the Assyrian conquest had carried off the entire population.

Joseph and Mary's journey to Bethlehem for the census would have been either seventy miles direct, over the mountains, or 100 miles via the gentler coastal route. Though tradition has it that Mary rode a donkey, none is mentioned in the Bible. They might conceivably have traveled south by boat from the ancient port of Acco or from Herod the Great's modern port of Caesarea to Jaffa.

Although the roads they traveled may have been paved by the Romans to facilitate the movement of troops and supplies up and down the country, journeys were generally neither particularly agreeable nor safe. They risked being set upon by thieves or attacked by wild animals. There were lions, wolves, hyenas, and jackals in the hills. There were cheetahs, leopards, bears, and wild boar in the forests. If they went the longer way of the coast, however, they would probably have traveled in company with merchants and their caravans of camels, carrying textiles, spices, perfumes, balm, and myrrh, or with itinerant farm workers.

The Nativity is generally told with Mary giving birth to Jesus on the night of their arrival in

LOVE TRIANGLES

Bethlehem but the gospel accounts do not say this. She and Joseph may have arrived some time before. According to Luke she spent about three months with Elizabeth before returning to her house. All told she may have been on the road for a further month, going to and from Elizabeth's home near Jerusalem and traveling to Bethlehem. We can say with assurance that she would have been obviously pregnant upon her arrival there.

The traditional December 25 birthdate is not mentioned in the Bible. It was arbitrarily chosen by the Roman Catholic Church to coincide with Saturnalia, a pagan festival that marked the visible renewal of the sun after the winter solstice on December 21.

It does not seem likely that Caesar Augustus would have required "all the world" to travel for the purposes of the census in the winter. In Israel, the former rains in November and the latter rains in March can cause devastating flash floods and other parts of the Roman Empire would have been deep in snow.

Since everything Jesus did was connected to Jewish tradition, festivals, and prophecy, I like to think that His birth was the same. Seemingly we have a clue to the correct timing of Jesus' birth in Luke 1:26, which tells us that the angel Gabriel was sent to Mary in the sixth month. It would help if we knew which sixth month he was talking about, the Roman or the Jewish calendar.

The sixth month in the Roman Julian calendar would give us a June conception date and a birth in

March or possibly April. Passover would have been a fitting time for His birth. Shepherds and their flocks are included in Luke's account, foreshadowing Jesus' role as both Shepherd and Lamb.

The Jewish calendar consists of some twelve-month and some "pregnant years" of thirteen months. We do not know whether Jesus' birth year was a pregnant year or not. The first month is Nissan in the spring, when Passover occurs, and the sixth month, *Tishri*, is the season of the High Holy Days: *Rosh haShana*, Yom Kippur, Sukkot, and *Simchat Torah*. It would be really special if the annunciation coincided with any of these festivals. Rosh haShana, Jewish New Year, celebrates new beginnings, although it does not actually mark the new year. This festival was named *Yom Teruah*, "the Day of Trumpets," in Leviticus 23, which implies an appropriate celebration of heralding. The Day of Atonement is about redemption from sin, while Tabernacles demonstrates the fragility of life, and "Joy in the Torah" celebrates God's given word.

Conception in Tishri, around September, would result in a June birth. Shavuot, Pentecost, falls in *Sivan*, a most fitting time for Jesus to be born since it would mark the beginning of events that come full circle with His ascension at Pentecost.

However, this would not be a good time of year for Caesar to call farm laborers away from their harvesting. A better time would be during the small hiatus between gathering in and plowing for the next season. Birth during the Pilgrimage Festival of Tabernacles fits that bill. ChristianAnswers.com suggests that Michael may have been the mighty angel who came to announce the birth of Jesus to the shepherds watching their flocks. The Feast of Michaelmas is on September 29, around the time of Tabernacles. John 1:14 also says, "And the Word became flesh and dwelt (literally 'tabernacled') among us." Tabernacles, in the fall, seems perhaps the most likely season for Jesus' birth.

A Tabernacles birth would indicate conception around *Tu b'Shevat*, the festival of first fruits and of trees, which usually falls in January. It is customary in Israel to gift beautifully-presented dried fruits and nuts at this time. In Jesus' day the festival was marked by the bringing of first fruits from newly-maturing young trees to the temple. Could the Virgin Mary also be viewed as a first-fruit offering to God?

There is an alternative explanation for Luke's reference to the sixth month. He could have been referring to the sixth month of Elizabeth's pregnancy. In Luke 1:36 the angel tells Mary, "Even Elizabeth your relative is going to have a child in her old age, and she who was said to be unable to conceive is in her sixth month." Many Bible translations are so convinced of Luke's meaning that they open chapter one this way: "In the sixth month of Elizabeth's pregnancy . . ."

One thing we can say is that God's timing for Jesus' birth was, as always, perfect. Jesus was born during the reign of Herod the Great, a puppet ruler of Israel, under the Roman Empire. Throughout His life and beyond His death and resurrection, Israel would remain subject to Rome. The Jews may have hated the Roman occupation, but communications were never better.

The Jewish disciples Jesus would surround Himself with were able to take His message to the Gentile world via the international network of Jewish synagogues that existed throughout the Roman Empire.

They reached them through straight, paved roads that the Romans developed over more than 50,000 miles, to serve the armed forces and trade. They reached them by sea. There was freedom of movement and, despite the dangers of shipwreck, opportunities to travel, both overland and by sea, would not be equaled for eighteen centuries.

Chapter 9 — Christmas with Gas Masks in the Land of Jesus

"But my righteous one will live by faith. And I take no pleasure in the one who shrinks back" (Hebrews 10:38).

By the 20th century, Haifa, where I was living during my second Christmas in Israel, had become a major seaport and the destination of choice for boatloads of Jewish immigrants pouring in from all over the world. Nowadays they come mainly by plane, as I did. Only luxury cruise liners, some as big as cities, would dock alongside the cargo ships far below my kitchen window. But not in winter; not at Christmas.

If our apartment, with its thick stone walls and high ceilings, was refreshingly cool in summer, it was positively chilly in winter. December 2010 found me shivering. The warmest place was in bed, opposite the only heater, with the blanket pulled up over my nose.

Outside in the streets they were wearing

mittens. Butch, from minus-minus temperatures in Canada, laughed. The weather really wasn't that cold, nothing like it could get in Jerusalem or Bethlehem.

We didn't go to Bethlehem that year either. I think perhaps Butch would have liked to go, but I don't feel we missed out. I had passed through, in the 1980s, before I believed in Yeshua and before the wall was built. My memories were of a shabby little town with a surly Arab population.

The Christian population of Haifa was large enough for the municipality to have placed an avant-garde Christmas tree on the main traffic circle in the middle of the German Colony, at the intersection of Allenby and Ben Gurion. It appeared to be made of recycled, clear plastic water bottles.

The only Christmas tree we'd seen the previous year in Tel Aviv/Jaffa had been in the volunteers' lounge at Beit Immanuel. The leadership had been hesitant about letting us have one, and the decision to go ahead had been presented as a big deal, for which we should be grateful. I think, in their minds, they were worried they might turn Beit Immanuel from Messianic into mainstream Christian.

The only public decorations in town were near the beach, a giant *Chanukiyah*, a nine-branched candlestick on which electric candles flickered to celebrate the festival of Chanukah. I was not able to find Christmas cards anywhere in the vicinity and had to resort to sending e-cards. That year, Christmas Day fell on a Friday, which was an

LOVE TRIANGLES

ordinary working day for all, including us, the volunteers.

In Haifa, by contrast, the balconies of our Christian Arab neighbors flashed illuminated reindeer and Santas and the shops were full of Christmassy things. We bought a tree with bulbs and jolly lights that blinked through their fast-slow sequence in our living room.

Christmas that year fell on the Sabbath, so no one was working. We got to worship and give thanks. There was a lot to be thankful for. Although Or haCarmel kept itself constantly on a war footing, storing plentiful supplies of food and clothing in a large shelter, we were living in relatively peaceful times.

The sirens kicked in one day when no practice had been announced that I knew about. I was on a Skype call to my son, Simon, at the time. I looked out the window. No one was running or abandoning cars for the shelters.

"Hold on a sec," I said.

I dialed Butch's cellphone. He was with his boss, who told him it was an improperly prepared drill. I guess everyone else thought so too because life was carrying on as normal.

It was a relief to know that I didn't have just sixty seconds to prepare for an incoming missile. Modern apartments have to be built with their own internal shelters, but ours, being well over 100 years old, didn't have one and there was no shelter nearby.

I had been through the English version of the

Guide to Emergency Preparedness that the Home Front Command of Israel had kindly issued me. I now knew that "being protected means being prepared." I had been to the post office to get my government-issue gasmask.

The safest place for me would be in the inner hallway, close to the kitchen but not too close to its glass door and windows. I would need to gather water from the refrigerator, the gasmask I kept in the bedroom, my cellphone from my purse, and the laptop I also kept in my bedroom. The guide always lay close by it. It gave emergency contact numbers. The laptop and telephone would help me receive news updates if I should become isolated.

I tried a dummy run. In sixty seconds I could grab all four items and even some food and throw myself down on the marble floor tiles in the hallway. It would have been better, I thought, as my bottom chilled, if I could have grabbed a blanket too. Maybe I would have time to tug one off the bed. It was then I remembered I hadn't closed doors and windows as the guide stipulated.

Thumbing through it, I saw I'd also missed bringing:
- Batteries for the laptop and phone
- Enough water: "A 3-day supply is recommended."
- Flashlight and batteries
- A first aid kit
- A fire extinguisher
- Games, newspapers and books to pass the time

LOVE TRIANGLES

- Important documents
- Medications

I had no chance of getting all that together in sixty seconds and certainly could not just leave it all piled in the narrow hallway for us to trip over.

The guide promised that, should the need arise, we would be instructed by the Home Front Command as to how to seal a room ahead of an expected chemical missile attack. We were advised on the order to do things in if the alarm sounded or an explosion was heard. We were first to finish sealing the room, don our gasmasks, and then stay put until given the all-clear via the media.

Earthquakes were another danger that was long overdue. In case of one of these, we were to do the opposite and run outside, as far away from the building as we could.

Having experienced neither, I wondered whether it might be hard to tell the difference. It all seemed so weird and impossible that I told God I was giving it up to Him. I also thanked Him over and over for peace. Before Christmas two tragic events that sent a breath of vulnerability down our necks would make us all the more grateful for His protection.

The first was close to home. On the morning of December 2, 2010, when I was not working, Butch, who was on the roof of Or haCarmel painting, saw smoke rising from Carmel Forest that we drove through going to and from work. This forest is a vast UNESCO International Bioreserve with unique Aleppo pine found nowhere else in the world.

Butch went to the office and fetched David Davis's secretary to come up on the roof to take a look. A small crowd assembled. As flames and billows of smoke began to shoot into the air, the secretary called the fire department.

A fourteen-year-old Druze boy and his friend had lit a shisha pipe. An absence of rain had left the trees and foliage tinder dry. Some leaves had caught alight and, in a flash, the fire was out of control. The boys ran.

It would rage, unstoppable, for four days at the top of Mount Carmel. The final death toll would be forty-four, making it the deadliest fire in Israeli history. The victims were young prison service officer cadets and their superiors, including the female chief of Haifa's police. A volunteer firefighter in his teens also died as well as the bus driver. They had been on their way to help evacuate a prison holding 500 prisoners.

On his way downhill, heading home, Butch passed the cortege of bus and the cars following it, climbing Carmel's twisting roads.

Minutes later, a tree, felled by the fire, would trap the bus in a fireball that would cause the driver to lose control. As he tried to make a U-turn on the narrow road, the bus caught fire. The cadets tried to escape by breaking through the back door, but the intense heat had soldered it closed. Those able to get out and flee jumped into a ravine beside the road. As they did so, the blaze came up to engulf them in a fiery inferno. A passing driver stopped to pick up the only survivors, an officer and two cadets, and drove them through the fire to safety.

Israeli Prime Minister, Binyamin Netanyahu, took charge of operations at Haifa University. Planes and firefighters worked around the clock to try and douse the flames. Israeli troops were mobilized. Heavy ground equipment from nearby military bases, including firetrucks, water tanks, cranes, and bulldozers were called in.

Fighting the fire appeared for the longest time to be a losing battle. Israel called on other countries for help. Many responded positively, including the Palestinian Authority.

Or haCarmel was put on high evacuation alert along with the rest of the population of Isifiya, the Druze village where it was located. More than 17,000 people were evacuated, including a kibbutz, several towns and villages, Haifa University, and the prison. Our Sudanese refugees and their children plus the staff and volunteers packed and waited. Although the order to leave never came, the refugees were moved to a location farther down Mount Carmel as a precaution. Later our congregation would try and help those who'd lost their homes pick up the pieces.

An estimated 1.5 million trees were destroyed and more than 12,000 acres of land were burned. Our morning and evening drives were transformed. The trees that we passed had lost their foliage. Their naked trunks and limbs were blackened. They reached angular arms towards us like charred and pleading ghosts of the dead.

The catastrophe demonstrated how seriously underequipped Israel was to fight major fires. The country had, proportionally, only one-quarter the firemen and firetrucks of Western countries and only a fraction of the fire retardants it needed, incredible statistics for a country that expects to come under missile fire.

To make matters worse, it would later emerge that the International Fellowship of Christians and Jews, which raises money for Israel among Christian supporters in North America, had provided Israel with eight new firefighting vehicles shortly before the fire. Rabbi Yechiel Eckstein, founder of the fellowship, maintained that contributions from non-Jewish sources were being rejected solely for religious reasons. It is not clear whether their gift of trucks had been commissioned or not. What is known is that further planned donations of vehicles did not take place because of the frosty reception the gift had received from the then ultra-Orthodox Minister of the Interior.

This same minister has been accused of employing illegal methods to investigate Aliyah applications of Jews suspected of Christian sympathies. He has since been replaced.

Later that same month, news came through that a woman I felt connected to through CMJ, the Church's Ministry among Jewish People, had been attacked by Arabs while out for a walk near Jerusalem. Her name was Kristine Luken. Her friend and walking companion, Kay Wilson, was badly wounded and left for dead. Kristine died.

LOVE TRIANGLES

I had been reading quite a lot about her in the CMJ newsletter over the previous twelve months. An American, she was hired by CMJ UK as their ministry staffer following a Skype interview while she was still in the USA. She demonstrated such a passion for the organization's work that, after interviewing her, the leadership would have no other. The struggle was then on to get her a working visa for the UK, which involved demonstrating that no British national could do the job as well.

CMJ managed to get Kristine her visa and she duly moved to Nottingham, England, a few months before her death. She and Kay met in Poland during the summer, as Kay, a British born Israeli tour guide, was leading a group around the concentration camps there.

They arranged to hike together in Israel during the Christmas holiday. They were attacked on December 18, 2010, while walking in the Mata Forest near the town of Beit Shemesh, west of Jerusalem, by two Arab men armed with a long, serrated knife. Kay fought back with her pocketknife, but she was no match for them.

After robbing them, the men held the two women at knifepoint with their hands tied behind their backs. Kay communicated that they were part of a tour group that would soon be returning, but after half an hour, it became obvious to the men this was not the case. It was then that hostage-taking turned into an execution. Kristine was murdered before Kay's eyes.

Kay later told police, "I realized he was going to behead me. I tried to keep silent. It was tough because the beatings were hard, but I tried to play dead."

Kay was stabbed thirteen times and sustained many broken bones as well as a punctured diaphragm and lungs. Weak from her injuries, she tried to move to the forest trail, hoping to be discovered after the assassins fled. Barefoot and bleeding, with her hands still tied behind her, she staggered over 1,200 meters to a parking lot, where a family saw her and called the emergency services.

"I just wanted to sleep and felt as though I was about to collapse," she said. "But I knew I could not fall asleep. I couldn't find my way and it was very difficult for me to breathe, but I had to make a switch in my head and think positive."

Kristine's bound and stabbed body was found the next morning after police combed the forests. A memorial service was later held for her at Christ Church, part of CMJ, in Jerusalem's Old City.

Her family said, "She went boldly where she believed God wanted her to go."

CMJ UK director, Robin Aldridge, praised her dedication and said, "She radiated goodness that came from the inner core of her being."

Her body was returned to the USA for burial.

The DNA on Kay's pocketknife led police to dismantle a Palestinian terror cell near Hebron. The attackers confessed and several other members of the cell were arrested, confessing to the murder of

LOVE TRIANGLES

an Israeli woman earlier that year and to other stabbing, rape, and shooting attacks. During their trial, the men declared that their goal was murdering Jews.

Kristine was someone I would sooner or later have met. I know, from the resolute way she had gone for the job she wanted, that she was someone I would have liked and perhaps become friends with.

Until then, it had seemed to me that some of the staff at Or haCarmel exaggerated to outsiders the danger of living here. These events changed my attitude.

I had lived in London for twenty or more years, never knowing when an IRA bomb might explode beside me. This was different. Israel was a much more intimate place, where the dead were known and close. It was depressing to think that seemingly nowhere in the Land had been spared its violent story, ancient or modern. The Sea of Galilee, as we shall see, was no exception to that rule. Yet it always felt to me like a place of peace.

Chapter 10 — On the Shores of Galilee

"The Lord is my shepherd, I lack nothing. He makes me lie down in green pastures, He leads me beside quiet waters, He refreshes my soul. He guides me along the right paths for His name's sake" (Psalm 23:1-3).

From the summit of Arbel National Park, I could see all the Sea of Galilee, shaped like King David's harp, from which its Hebrew name, *Kinneret*, is derived.

To me this is the loveliest place on earth. In spring the mountains surrounding the Sea are a vivid green. Come summer they are fired ginger by the intense, dry heat. On this June day a blue mist blurred the line where the blue water met the blue hills all around. There was a stillness and a silence in the atmosphere, as if the world were holding its breath.

Butch's son, Mitchel, visiting from Canada, was walking with us on the last part of the Jesus Trail that leads from Nazareth to Capernaum. We felt privileged to be seeing what Jesus saw and to be walking where He walked.

Our descent took us most of the day. Parts were vertical and involved picking our way down steep stone paths and scrambling down sheer cliff faces by means of metal ladders. Always before us was the Sea of Galilee, the lowest freshwater lake in the world.

Peering inside the entrance of one of a series of caves, we were startled to see several pairs of eyes glinting back at us. These were neither thieves nor the remnant of some holed-up crusader army, but cows, sheltering from the day's heat.

According to Josephus, the caves were the site of the Battle of Arbel in 37 BCE, when Galilean Zealots barricaded themselves in against Herod the Great's army. Committed Jews, the Zealots, favored armed rebellion against Roman control. The rebels had no chance against Herod's men who were lowered in baskets on ropes to pick them off with arrows and fiery brands. The Zealots were wiped out. Josephus recounts that one old man killed his wife and seven sons, then threw their bodies into the gorge before jumping in after them to his death.

Some fifty or so years after this massacre, Mount Arbel would be the backdrop to much of Jesus' teaching and miracles. At least one of His disciples, Peter, was a known Zealot (Luke 6:15).

Given the Jewish expectation that the Messiah would be a great warrior king, it is not surprising, in such a setting and with Zealots in His entourage, that people assumed Jesus had come to lead them in an uprising. He would indeed shake things up but in ways they could not have imagined.

The dramatic end to Jesus' ministry on earth would come in Jerusalem. He predicted this when He said, "Surely no prophet can die outside Jerusalem" (Luke 13:33). In Nazareth His life was *yom-yom*, "everyday". Before His ministry began, no one there, except perhaps Mary and Joseph, knew Him for the Messiah He would become. It is on the shores of the Sea of Galilee that we see Jesus at His most relaxed, enjoying the work God had for Him.

He healed by the Sea of Galilee. "Jesus went throughout Galilee, teaching in their synagogues, proclaiming the good news of the Kingdom, and healing every disease and sickness among the people. News about Him spread all over Syria, and people brought to Him all who were ill with various diseases, those suffering severe pain, the demon-possessed, those having seizures, and the paralyzed; and He healed them. Large crowds from Galilee, the Decapolis, Jerusalem, Judea and the region across the Jordan followed him" (Matthew 4:23-25).

Here, too, Jesus demonstrated, through example and vivid stories, God's message of love for us and how we were to pass that on. He revealed Himself a Master Storyteller. He taught about honesty, integrity, neighborliness, open-mindedness, and fair-mindedness. Though the characters were made up, the stories He told were true. We learn the lessons his listeners learned.

LOVE TRIANGLES

He illustrated good by demonstrating the bad that was in the world. Before the Prodigal Son became humble and sought forgiveness, he was annoyingly arrogant and selfish. We itch for him to see the light and change.

Jesus' settings were familiar to His listeners. The story of the sower is a Galilean agricultural story. He told it to a crowd on the shore as He stood in a boat on the Sea of Galilee. A sower hung a bag of seed around his neck and went out to sow it in handfuls. It may have been November, following the first rains. The grape and fig harvests were done, the olives gathered in, and the ground turned over, ready to receive the seed. The sower, who surely was Jesus Himself, dearly wanted all the seed fanning out from his fingers to take and grow into sturdy plants, but that wasn't how things would turn out.

Some seed would fall on the path and be eaten by the birds. Some would shoot up quickly on shallow soil or rocky ground, and the sun would scorch the leaves so they would wither. These shoots hadn't rooted properly. Other seed would fall among thorns that would choke the plants as they grew. Only the seed that fell on good soil would produce a good crop.

Jesus explained to His disciples (Matthew 13) that His story represented the different ways people received the message about God. The seed eaten by the birds represented folks stolen away to sin by Satan. The seed that sprang up on rocks stood for those who rejoiced to hear the message but fell away at the least sign of trouble. The seed choked by thorns were those people too worldly to stick with their faith. Those who heard the message and understood and accepted it would produce an abundant harvest.

This story was called a parable, from the Greek *parabole,* an illustration in the form of a brief fictional story. It is often thought that Jesus invented parables, but there are several in the Old Testament, such as the one told by Nathan to David in 2 Samuel 12. In Hebrew this type of storytelling is known as *mashal,* short stories with a moral lesson or religious allegory. Jewish tradition has it that King Solomon, that great and most wealthy and wise of kings, invented mashal and prior to that, no one could understand the Bible.

Here is one parable Jesus might have told in the orchards of Migdal. Migdal, which means "tower," lies at the foot of Mount Arbel, close to Capernaum. "Suppose one of you wants to build a tower. Won't you first sit down and estimate the cost to see if you have enough money to complete it? For if you lay the foundation and are not able to finish it, everyone who sees it will ridicule you, saying, 'This person began to build and wasn't able to finish'" (Luke 14:28-29).

The tower Jesus would have pointed to, to drive home His point, may have been for drying fish caught in the Sea of Galilee. Or Migdal may have been named for a vineyard watchtower or a tower for some other purpose, perhaps defensive.

LOVE TRIANGLES

Migdal is supposed to have given Mary Magdalene her name. The nickname Magdalene implied that she was from Migdal. She had joined Jesus' entourage after He healed her of seven demons, and became one of several women who supported Him financially and traveled around the country with Him (Luke 8:1-3).

She may not have been from Migdal at all but given the name because she was a "tower of strength" or simply because she was tall. The name may have been inspired by the three heavily fortified towers built by King Herod at Jerusalem's citadel, the highest point of the city. They were renowned for their beauty and referred to by Josephus as "the Women's Towers."

Around the bend from Migdal, on the northern shore of the Sea of Galilee, lies *Kfar Nahum*, the village of Nahum, commonly known as Capernaum. This includes Peter's house, which is covered by a church today. Close by it are evocative pillars and rubble carved with Jewish symbols, the remains of a 4th century synagogue that archaeologists have excavated. Recently they have discovered a 1st century synagogue beneath it. Jesus may have read from the Torah scroll and preached at this synagogue. It could be the one mentioned in this verse: "On a Sabbath Jesus was teaching in one of the synagogues" (Luke 13:10).

Capernaum lies beside a quiet crescent beach. From here, you can see almost to the distant southern tip of the sea. I have looked out and pictured Jesus—and Peter too—walking on the water (Matthew 14:22-33).

A terrible storm blew up as the disciples were heading back to Capernaum in their boat after a long day of ministry. Water that is like glass in the morning often turns choppy and angry later in the day. This storm was at night. Shortly before dawn they saw Jesus, who had left them to go away and pray alone, walking towards them on the water. They were terrified and thought they were seeing a ghost, but Jesus reassured them it really was Him.

"Come," He told Peter, who wanted to join him.

Bravely, Peter got out of the boat and splashed across the surface of the deep, thrilled to be walking on water. Then, as the wind whistled and whipped up the spray so that it lashed his flesh and eyes, his trust in Jesus wavered. In an instant, Peter sank to his thighs. His arms flailed. He was going under.

"Lord, save me!" he cried.

Rebuking him for his lack of faith, Jesus bent towards him and held out His hand. As they climbed into the boat together, the wind subsided.

"Truly you are the Son of God," the disciples said in wonder.

Their boat, or one like it, has been found, preserved for 2,000 years in Galilean mud, and restored. The Jesus Boat can now be viewed beside the Sea of Galilee.

Navigating the Sea of Galilee is not simple. A contemporary Galilee fishermen has stressed the importance of being "in tune with nature and watching for the little signs of what the lake is about to do." He says that when he fishes he feels "like a hunter." He fishes for St. Peter's fish. This is very much *the* local dish, eaten out-of-doors with French fries. It is actually tilapia.

The disciples' boat would have demanded a crew of at least five, four to row and one to manipulate the rudder oar at the back. They had to pull together to haul in heavy nets full of fish. Their livelihoods, and sometimes their very lives, depended on teamwork. No wonder Jesus recruited Galilean fishermen to work together to become fishers of people.

"As Jesus was walking beside the Sea of Galilee, He saw two brothers, Simon called Peter and his brother Andrew. They were casting a net into the lake, for they were fishermen. 'Come, follow me,' Jesus said, 'and I will send you out to fish for people.' At once they left their nets and followed him. Going on from there, He saw two other brothers, James son of Zebedee and his brother John. They were in a boat with their father Zebedee, preparing their nets. Jesus called them, and immediately they left the boat and their father and followed Him" (Matthew 4:18-22).

During the day that ended with Jesus walking on water, He shared two little fishes and five small loaves among 5,000 men, as well as women and children. There was plenty to go around and basketsful of leftovers. This is the only miracle, outside of the resurrection, that is told in all four Gospels.

A crowd had followed Jesus across to the other side of the lake and was growing hungry, which caused Him to wryly ask Philip to buy bread to feed them. Philip thought Him crazy. He retorted that it would cost half a year's wages to feed them all.

Andrew, a little hesitant perhaps, volunteered the information that a boy in the crowd had five loaves and two fishes. To his surprise, Jesus thought that would be just the thing. He had everyone sit down on the green grass, which tells us it was springtime, the prettiest time of year, when everything feels fresh and new. The air is not too hot then and there is often a warm breeze.

Raising His eyes to heaven, Jesus blessed the bread and fish and broke them into pieces for the disciples to hand out. It was divided among the multitude and twelve baskets were filled with the leftovers.

The boy with the bread and fish may have been biting his nails, wondering how angry his mom would be with him, only to find her in the crowd, eager to tell him of the miracle she had witnessed. He had no need to be concerned. There would be plenty to take home for Dad's supper too.

One morning, as I was taking a dip in the Sea of Galilee's cool water, I pictured the risen Jesus on the shore, watching His disciples returning, downcast from a poor night's fishing. I saw this as happening after the initial surge of converts at Pentecost. Things had become challenging. The Jews hated them for saying the Messiah had come, as large numbers of Jews still hate those who say

LOVE TRIANGLES

so today.

"I am going fishing," Peter told the others.

He stopped fishing for people and returned to what he knew. Some of the disciples went with him (John 21).

Would they, in spite of the empty tomb, the eyewitness reports that Jesus was risen, and their own encounters with Him be like the seed that sprang up on rocks, rejoicing to hear the message but falling away at the least sign of trouble?

Jesus lit a charcoal fire and began cooking fish. He also had some bread. As their boat came closer, He called out to them, "Friends, haven't you any fish?"

"No!" they cried. They did not know it was Jesus. He told them to cast their nets on the right side of the boat. Clearly they had been fishing in all the wrong places just before this because, when they fished where Jesus said, they caught so many fish they could not land them.

Peter, realizing who it was, jumped into the water and swam towards Him. Meanwhile the others rowed ashore, dragging the net that was overflowing with fish.

"Come and have breakfast," Jesus said and asked them to add to the feast by bringing some of the fish they had just caught. They did so, counting 153 large fish in all. The whole catch had been safely landed without a single tear in the net.

"When they had finished eating, Jesus said to Simon Peter, 'Simon son of John, do you love me more than these?'

"'Yes, Lord,' he said. 'You know that I love you.'

"Jesus said, 'Feed my lambs.'

"Again Jesus said, 'Simon son of John, do you love me?'

"He answered, 'Yes, Lord, You know that I love you.'

"Jesus said, 'Take care of my sheep.'

"The third time He said to him, 'Simon son of John, do you love me?'

"Peter was hurt because Jesus asked him the third time, 'Do you love me?' He said, 'Lord, You know all things; You know that I love You.'

"Jesus said, 'Feed my sheep'" (John 21:15-17).

Then He got to His feet and said, "Follow me."

Peter got up and followed Him.

Jesus wasn't about to allow Peter to become the one that got away. By bringing him back, the good seed that He had sown on fertile soil would produce an abundant harvest, "a hundred, sixty or thirty times what was sown" (Matthew 13:8).

Looking on, I wondered where, in all of Israel, I might produce any kind of a harvest.

Chapter 11 – Why Must I Choose Between Jesus and His Jewish Homeland?

"Do not be afraid; keep on speaking, do not be silent. For I am with you, and no one is going to attack and harm you, because I have many people in this city" (Acts 18:9-10).

I'd had my eye on the village of Kiryat Tivon as a place to live. Not only was it handy for our work at Or HaCarmel, it was also cute and quaint, with a little café where the local community would hang out. When we chatted to people about living there, local residents gathered around our table to enthuse about their amateur dramatics group and other activities.

After viewing a couple of properties, we left it however. The prospect of tiptoeing around, hiding my Messianic identity, turned me off. I just couldn't stand the idea of other Jews looking at me sideways.

We considered moving to a *Moshav*. *Moshavim* are former agricultural cooperatives. One we liked was near the Sea of Galilee, but I couldn't see us fitting in there either.

There were Christian areas, like Poriya Illit, which has a stunning view over the Sea of Galilee. Something was holding me back from these too, a reluctance to lock myself into a quasi-ghetto, set apart from the nation I was embracing. This was already happening at work, where I was surrounded by English-speaking Jewish believers.

I would have preferred to sell what we had in England and buy a place of our own in Israel, but that seemed risky on several fronts, not the least of which was the possibility of getting thrown out of the country for being a traitor who believed in Yeshua.

In the end we signed a lease for another year in our Haifa apartment. It was a pretty apartment, airy in summer, with a lovely view of the Mediterranean. A young, Egyptian-looking cat with a long, elegant neck had started to wander onto and off of the balcony. We named her Tabitha.

On May 24, 2011, Butch and I hunkered down in the living room to watch Prime Minister Netanyahu's address to the U.S. Congress in Washington, DC. One of the first things he said was this: "You don't need to export democracy to Israel. We have already got it." This got his listeners to their feet, applauding. It was a good beginning.

Quoting writer George Elliot's prediction of 100 years earlier, Netanyahu went on to say that, in an area of intolerance and religious persecution, Israel stood out "like a bright star of freedom amidst the despotism of the East." Although there were nascent bids for democracy in some neighboring countries, Israel was the one anchor in the Middle East; only a tiny percentage of the world's Arabs enjoyed the benefits of true democracy and they were Israeli citizens.

Bibi, as Binyamin Netanyahu is affectionately known in Israel, was composed, even jovial. I loved how he was talking. I was proud of him and proud to be Israeli. He highlighted the many dangers of the violence pursued by the governments of some Middle Eastern countries and condemned the utter silence of some on-looking nations or, worse still, the blame directed at Israel by others for defending itself.

"Not you. Not America," he said.

There was further applause.

Netanyahu moved on to talk of his commitment and that of his immediate predecessors to a Palestinian state alongside a Jewish state, even at the cost of giving up tracts of land that were the ancestral homeland of the Jews. The Palestinian people had roots there, too, he said, and the right to become a "free, liberal, and independent people, living in their own state."

If this had not yet come about, it was solely because the Palestinians could not accept the existence of a Jewish state. "This is what this conflict is about."

The Palestinian state had to become a partner for peace, not the annihilation of Israel, he argued.

Compromise by Israel would be required to achieve this, but on this Netanyahu was firm: "Israel will not return to the indefensible boundaries of 1967."

I was stirred.

Earlier that month, we had celebrated Independence Day in Israel for the second year running. We had been out and about, watching military displays and had followed nostalgic television programs that included songs that remembered the formation of the State in 1948. For several weeks before this, we had flown Israeli flags attached to our car, even replacing those that had gone missing while parked overnight on our Arab Christian street.

This country was created with the vision of Israel's beautiful national anthem: to live in freedom in a land of our own. I embraced this vision that played a major role in bringing me to want to make Aliyah. But what Netanyahu said next changed everything for me.

"As for Jerusalem, only a democratic Israel has protected the freedom of worship for all faiths in the city. Throughout the millennial history of the Jewish capital, the only time that Jews, Christians, and Moslems could worship freely, could have unfettered access to their holy sites, has been during Israel's sovereignty of Jerusalem."

He was arguing powerfully for his point, that Jerusalem must never again be divided. Although what he was declaring to the world was truth—Jews, Christians, and Moslems could follow their faith in Israel—it was a million miles from the

LOVE TRIANGLES

whole truth.

The unspoken truth was in the experience of a member of Jews for Jesus. We'll call him John. John would like to come and live in Israel. As a Jew, he would like to make Aliyah. However, unless he can reverse the ten-year ban on coming to Israel that was the result of his last visit to the country, he will not even be able to begin that process.

John's evangelizing on the streets of Israel landed him in a prison cell. Since evangelizing adults is not illegal in Israel, the charge could only be one of disturbing the peace. Anyone looking back over police records is unlikely to identify the prejudicial stance of the Israeli police in this matter.

The unspoken truth was also in the experience of Michael Dearington, an evangelical Christian with permanent residency in Israel, who voluntarily served in the IDF. Through his service he qualified for citizenship. However, the Ministry of the Interior delayed his application interminably based on reasons that were religiously discriminatory and false rumors circulated by ultra-Orthodox Jews that Michael was engaged in illegal missionary activities. The truth was that he helped other Christian Zionists like himself prepare for IDF service.

After two years of waiting in vain for a decision, the Jerusalem Institute of Justice, headed by American Israeli Calev Myers, a Messianic believer, took on the case and successfully petitioned Israel's Supreme Court of Justice on Michael's behalf, requesting that there be no further delays to the granting of the citizenship that was his legal right.

The unspoken truth is in the invented setbacks and postponements of residency rights suffered by non-Jewish spouses of Messianic Jews like our friends Katja and Yaron, who eventually gave up in disgust and moved to Katja's native Germany. Germany has welcomed Yaron. He has trained for the clergy and the couple now have two beautiful children.

Netanyahu was presenting the State of Israel as the only modern democracy in the Middle East. But a true democracy allows all its citizens freedom of faith and Israel wasn't doing that. The nation whose vision I heartily embraced had a policy of waging war on Jewish believers like me. Being an outcast broke my heart.

Though I yearned to be guided by these words: "For the Spirit God gave us does not make us timid, but gives us power, love and self-discipline" (2 Timothy 1:7), I think I knew at that moment I couldn't stay.

I had no peace about it. I remembered how God said to Patriarch Isaac, "Live in the Land where I tell you to live. Stay in this Land for a while, and I will be with you and will bless you. For to you and your descendants I will give all these lands and will confirm the oath I swore to your father Abraham" (Genesis 26:2-3). Here I was, thinking of leaving.

LOVE TRIANGLES

I felt too uncomfortable, despite all that there was to love. The loveliness came from being deeper in the Spirit than I had ever been before. Picturing Jesus in His Jewish homeland, my faith had bloomed like the red anemones that beautify the Land every February. I had never felt closer to God. But I had also never felt more of a fake. To me, sneaking around constituted a fail in my bid to be as like Jesus as I could be.

Though I was no longer listening attentively, Prime Minister Netanyahu's address continued. He talked of a peace that must be anchored in security, where missiles did not—and could not—rain down on Israel's people and its children.

I had never experienced such things, although some had told me how terrifying attacks could be. I did not have children in the IDF, though Messianic parents had told me of their misgivings every time their kid returned to base. Israelis of my own generation had clammed up when questioned how service in the IDF had been for them, saying only, "It was bad."

Netanyahu finished his address by affirming that Israel was prepared to sit down and negotiate peace, but not with a Palestinian government whose charter said, "Kill the Jews everywhere you find them."

This set me to thinking about anti-Semitism. Even if it is sometimes hard to put your finger on, you know it is there:

• When a Canadian student complains someone "jewed" him (i.e.: tricked him out of some money); the culprit may or may not have been Jewish

- When a French Jew introduces himself as "Israëlite" rather than "Juif"
- In the way you avoid revealing that you are Jewish to new people you meet.

How would I feel returning to that insidious kind of prejudice? The answer was that it was a life I knew how to deal with.

My prayers in the days that followed were full of questions about God's will for us. Family considerations came to the fore. Butch's mother had been very sick in Canada. My eldest son and his family had visited. Fun time spent with them made me realize just how much I missed having family close by.

I wanted my family to share in the loving God I had found. To keep the truth to myself was to deprive them. But they didn't want to hear. None of them did. At least if I were where they were, I could model what I stood for.

The Jewish people in Israel didn't want to hear either. If we were to stay, there had to be a purpose to it. Didn't there? Surely our work at Or haCarmel, where Butch sweated while painting the roof and I typed, weren't all we were intended to do for the Kingdom? Or was that arrogance?

On the day we made Aliyah, I had seen God's will in it. Now I was less certain. For months I had been asking for the strength to stay. In the end it wasn't that I was hearing Him tell me to leave as much as I was no longer hearing Him say, "Stay."

LOVE TRIANGLES

Butch didn't want us to go, but he left the decision up to me. We began the process of *Yoridah*, "going down." We sold the things we had bought or shipped them to the UK. We did a lot of form filling to discontinue all the things we were signed up for.

We went sadly, with our heads hung low. We had failed. We were abandoning everyone, breaking the human chain. We were becoming defectors in a different way. We were sorry to be leaving the friends we had made at work and our home group at Beit Eliyahu. Sam, its leader, had lived back and forth between the States and Israel, which encouraged us that maybe we too might return one day.

Feeling a calling, he originally made Aliyah in the 70s. "I just knew in my heart," he told me.

After a couple of years, however, he left, only to return twenty-nine years later, "after I grew up in the Lord; my kids were of age and my mom had passed."

Coming back was a faith decision, made in spite of a 2006 reconnaissance trip that had yielded "nothing to like in the natural. The one thing that I did like, and always have, was meeting people from all over the world." We had loved that about Israel too.

Five and a half years on, doors have opened for Sam to teach the grace message in Israel.

"I know that I am supposed to be here and yet, with what God has taught me, I do not feel like I totally fit in even with the Messianic Jews because I have learned freedom through the finished work of the cross."

By that he meant what he taught, what we had loved to learn at home group, namely, "For sin shall no longer be your master, because you are not under the law, but under grace" (Romans 6:14). This was not accepted by all believing Jews in Israel. Many still slavishly followed Jewish law in the same way as non-believing Jews.

Sam didn't fit into Israel's mainstream Jewish community and didn't quite fit into the Messianic community either. And neither did we. Yet he was staying and we were not.

Chapter 12 — Dew in the Desert

"I will rejoice in doing them good and will assuredly plant them in this land with all my heart and soul" (Jeremiah 32:41).

Since our departure, there have been hints that Israel outside of the Supreme Court and the Ministry of the Interior is changing for the better. The secular media have begun running favorable pieces about Messianic Jews and incidents of persecution have made the front page.

Knut Hoyland, of the Caspari Study Center in Jerusalem, comments, "At least we see that believers are being asked to explain who they are, what they believe in, why they are here, how they can be Israeli and believe in Jesus and be given an opportunity to tell their story and share their testimony."

In January 2012, Prime Minister Netanyahu demonstrated the high value he places on the relationship between Christians and Jews by appointing two goodwill ambassadors to Jewish and Christian communities around the world.

International Christian broadcaster and journalist, Earl Cox, a Christian advocate for Israel and head of Israel Always, is one. "Doors which have been traditionally closed tight to Christians have now begun to open," he says, "as Israel's leaders, religious and governmental, come to recognize that the evangelical Christian community of the world is the best friend Israel has in all the world."

The second ambassador is New York City born Rabbi Shlomo Riskin, a prominent and controversial figure in modern orthodoxy and founder of the Israeli settlement of Efrat in the West Bank. Israel cannot but feel ambiguous as it extends the hand of friendship to dreaded missionaries. What swayed Rabbi Riskin in favor of Christians, however, was the fact that they kept coming to Israel, even when the bombs were falling. This has led him to found the Center for Jewish-Christian Understanding. Another consideration is that charitable giving by Christians pours an estimated $210 million a year into Israel-related ministries.

Along with Christian broadcasting notables like Jay Sekulow, John Hagee, and Pat Roberston, Rabbi Riskin has endorsed a new Christian venture on the shores of the Sea of Galilee, the Galilean Resort and Spa. It was founded by Anne Ayalon, who was raised an evangelical Christian and converted to Judaism. She is the wife of former Israeli Deputy Foreign Minister and Ambassador to the U.S., Danny Ayalon. The resort's vocation is to help Christians "experience Israel through Bible study, educational courses, cultural programs, and life-changing experiences."

Another boon to reconciliation is the recently created Galilee Center for Studies in Jewish-Christian Relations. The Center supports Jewish-Christian engagement in Israel by organizing undergraduate programs, summer programs, and research bursaries. They are open to all, Jews and Christians, clergy and lay people, Israelis and overseas visitors.

The fact that this center sits within the Max Stern Jezreel Valley College, a regular Israeli college of 5,000 students, is especially encouraging because it confirms the subject of Jewish-Christian Relations as mainstream learning and sends a signal to the world's Jews that Christianity, the Gospels, and the life of Jesus are no longer taboo subjects, too sinful and dangerous to even mention. At the same time, the world's Christians are invited to the Center to explore Judaism, which was the practice of Jesus.

The opening of both these centers is timely. In the West there is a swing away from centuries of replacement theology that suggested God had reneged on His Old Testament promises and changed His mind about His choice of the Jews as His Chosen People and Israel as His Land in favor of the Christian Church.

There is growing recognition within Christianity of what seems to me to be obvious, namely, that Jesus' coming was the fulfilment of God's plan, foretold in the Hebrew Bible.

Rabbi Riskin applauds what he calls this "sea change." "Christians are sincerely trumpeting the call that God remains faithful to His initial covenant with Israel and that the biblical prophecy is continually being fulfilled through the people of Israel living in its covenanted land."

A further manifestation of entente was in the previously mentioned keynote address of Ron Lauder, President of the World Jewish Congress, at International Christian Embassy Jerusalem's 2014 Annual Conference in Jerusalem, in which he declared, "Israel has no better friends in the world than you. We know that you have watched out for us and we will always watch out for you."

He pointed out that, unlike the Middle East and Africa, Israel's Christian holy sites are protected and its Christian population growing, not shrinking. Christians in Israel currently number around 158,000, 2 percent of the population. They are growing, but at a slower rate than other sectors, just 1.3 percent per year, compared to Jewish growth of 1.8 percent and Moslem growth of 2.5 percent. Currently some 80 percent of Israeli Christians are Arabs, denominationally Orthodox, Catholic, and Messianic.

There are around 20,000 Messianic Jews, with 130-150 Messianic congregations plus Messianic home churches. Back in 1948, "twelve Jews who believed in Jesus could be counted," the Baptist Press reports. In 1987, that number was 3,000. By 1997, it had grown to 5,000.

LOVE TRIANGLES

Further surges are anticipated as more and more Israeli-born Jews and Russian immigrants turn to Jesus. Their numbers are swelled by those from the West who manage to immigrate by slipping under the radar of the Ministry of the Interior, American Jews like Eddie and Jackie Santoro who made Aliyah in 1997.

After learning Hebrew, they founded *Ahavat Yeshua* Congregation in Jerusalem in 2006. Starting with twenty people, they had over 100 by 2009 and have not stopped growing since. Ahavat Yeshua is a member of the Messianic umbrella organization *Tikkun International,* which supports and equips congregations, ministries, and leaders in America, Israel, and throughout the world.

The mushrooming numbers of Israeli Messianic believers is part of a worldwide trend. Estimates range as high as 350,000 for the world, roughly the number of Jews living in the UK today. Messianics represent some 2.5 percent of the total Jewish world population of around 14 million. Joel Chernoff, CEO of Messianic Jewish Alliance of America, uses somewhat convoluted calculations to arrive at an estimated one million Messianic Jews in the world today.

"Jews are becoming believers in Yeshua," he confirms, adding that there are now some 800 Messianic Jewish congregations in the world, whereas in 1967 there were none.

Whatever the actual numbers, there is no denying that recognizing Jesus as the Jewish Messiah is a fast-growing trend worldwide.

Growth in the United States is sustained and phenomenal. Today there are approaching 450 Messianic congregations, over double the 150 recorded in 2013, figures that do not include home church fellowships. Fifty years ago there were maybe five. A 2013 survey by Pew Research Center showed there were about 159,000 Messianic Jews in the United States. Top cities are Manhattan, Miami, and Philadelphia.

One of the largest and oldest Messianic congregations in the world is *Beth Hallel* in Atlanta, Georgia. This congregation is typical of many others in having a mixed membership. "The congregation comes from many different backgrounds, including all branches of traditional Judaism as well as many denominations," Beth Hallel's Rabbi Robert Solomon says. "While the majority of our member families come from a Jewish background, we have a strong minority of non-Jewish members as well."

A new term has been coined to describe the often significant proportion of non-Jews who choose to join Messianic congregations: Messianic Gentiles.

Lael Osborne used to think that stories "about Moses and such" were not relevant to the church. "They were for Israel and we're not Israel."

Now she and husband, Matthew, keep the biblical feast days and avoid pork and shellfish. "I have been slowly but surely applying more and more of the Laws of God given to Moses because I love God and long to please Him," she says.

LOVE TRIANGLES

This is no easy thing for the young couple to do in their rural home province of New Brunswick, known as Canada's Bible Belt and steeped in traditional Christianity. There are few Jews and no Messianic congregations. Kosher food is not available.

"We try to follow as best we can what we find in the Scriptures," Matthew says. They do not feel morally obligated to keep rabbinic law.

Their practice has been inspired by Lael's parents, who belong to a Messianic home church, Iron Sharpens Iron, in Maine, USA, where the weekly Torah portions are studied alongside corresponding New Testament passages. The online programs of El Shaddai Ministries in Washington and Passion for Truth Ministries, Missouri, have also provided guidance.

Lael and Matthew have come to the conclusion that Paul's letters demonstrate that he considered the Law "holy, just, good, and righteous."

"It's not only the Torah and the feast days that I've become excited about," she continues. "I'm seeing Jesus all over the Old Testament in places I never expected to find Him."

She gives, as an example, Joseph's interpretation of his fellow prisoners' dreams in Genesis 40, linking the baker, who would die on a tree, to Jesus' crucifixion and the wine cupbearer, who was restored to his position, to the resurrection through the Last Supper. There, Jesus blessed bread and wine, the baker and the cupbearer's stock in trade, and asked the disciples to remember His broken body and blood.

Matthew believes that every mention of "the angel of the Lord" in the Old Testament is actually Jesus.

A lot of friends and family don't agree with what Lael and Matthew, the son of an Anglican minister, believe and practice.

"I don't question their salvation in the least," Lael says. Underlining that following the path they have chosen is a personal choice, she adds, "I see that I was missing out on a blessing before."

Despite the challenges, they remain enthusiastic. "We made a *menorah* at Christmas because I really like the image of Jesus as the servant candle. We called it *Christanukah*," Lael says. "The more I learn and the more I obey, the more I become captivated."

Unlike many others I interviewed for this book, I am able to use the Osbornes' real names because, in Canada, they are free to be themselves. Being a Jewish believer in Israel, it was not as easy to be myself.

Jackie Santoro of Ahavat Yeshua Congregation echoes my own feelings when she says, "I think probably the greatest challenge is that you always feel that the rest of society isn't accepting you. And so when you meet somebody and you want to talk to them and you want to tell them who you are, there's always that challenge of 'should I say something?'"

When I talked to native-born Israeli, Joshua Pex, he confirmed the dangers. "They could annul

LOVE TRIANGLES

your Aliyah. It's a threat that looms over you."

I asked him whether, as a Messianic Jew, he ever felt under threat.

"If you are born here, an Israeli, you are protected as a citizen," he said.

I told him I admired his courage in not slinking around and disguising his faith.

"Many places, people think you're a little bit strange, a bit different," he said. "Many people have never heard of anything like it when you tell them that, for me, Yeshua is the Messiah or that you read the New Testament. This is something outrageous."

He added, "You're careful, as you don't want to offend or upset people."

That was how I was—careful.

I thought of Jesus' admonition to His disciples when He sent them out like sheep among wolves to evangelize the people of Israel with their wits as their only weapon. He told them to be cunning as serpents while remaining innocent as doves (Matthew 10:16).

"Being Messianic, many people don't like it, but most people are pretty indifferent," Joshua continued. "They don't really care what you believe. There are doors that are closed. I have gotten used to it."

What he seemed to be saying was that being an outsider wasn't such a big deal.

"This is where we feel we should be and where God would want us to be." *We* included Joshua's Dutch-born wife, who made Aliyah, and their children.

Pastor Chuck Cohen of Intercessors for Prayer in Jerusalem feels the same way as Joshua: Israel is where he should be.

I had sought that feeling and not gotten there. I had made being an outsider a big deal and had shaken the dust from my feet.

Chuck Cohen confirmed that he was seeing a growing acceptance of Messianic Judaism in Israel. People were getting used to them, he maintained, as their numbers increased. He and his wife made Aliyah from the United States in 1989, the same year that the Beresfords lost their first appeal to the Supreme Court. (See Chapter 5.)

The process was not problem-free. They found the bureaucracy frustrating, finances challenging, and everything strange. Yet they have stayed, he says, because he came with this attitude: "I'm not here because I love Israel and its culture. I'm here because Yeshua wants me here and I love Him."

It is plain today that he does love Israel and has adopted its culture. His demeanor is also engagingly Israeli—aka, blunt. Pastor Chuck told me I should return to Israel. He believes it's where I belong.

Since hardly a week goes by that my husband and I don't discuss that eventuality, I suppose it could happen. If it did I would be surer of who I am and less caring of what everyone else thinks. But I don't have to be in Israel to love Jesus.

Of the Jewish exile in Babylon, Eugene Petersen wrote, "They found that God was not dependent on a place; He was not tied to familiar surroundings. The violent dislocation of the exile shook them out of their comfortable but reality-distorting assumptions and allowed them to see depths and heights that they had never even imagined before. They lost everything that they thought was important and found what was important: they found God."

What I received in Israel, a closeness to Jesus like never before, has remained with me in the Diaspora. I can meet with Him anywhere. He speaks to me everywhere. I have learned that I too must speak out.

Martin Luther King Jr. said, "Our lives begin to end the day we become silent about things that matter."

That was me—there, then. No more. This book is my beginning.

Prayers for Aliyah inspired by Chuck Cohen of Intercessors for Israel Ministry, (www.ifi.org.il)

- Thank You, Lord, for the increased numbers making Aliyah, especially from Ukraine and France.
- May they come quickly and not wait until it's too late.
- May the Israeli government prepare the land for Aliyah. "The desolate land will be cultivated instead of lying desolate in the sight of all who pass through it. They will say, 'This land that was laid waste has become like the garden of Eden; the cities that were lying in ruins, desolate and destroyed, are now fortified and inhabited'" (Ezekiel 36:34-35).
- Raise up people and ministries dedicated to bringing the Jewish people home.
- Renew the Jews' sense of belonging in the Land so they may be at home in their home.
- Remove the obstacles to Aliyah.
- Shake the Jews out of the comfortable little kingdoms they have built for themselves in the nations.
- Give us a Minister of Interior who has or who You can give a new heart for the Aliyah.
- Remove the heart of stone in the Ministry of Interior. "I will give you a new heart and put a new spirit in you; I will remove from you your heart of stone and give you a heart of flesh" (Ezekiel 36:26).
- Let there be a welcome for the Messianic Jews.

Glossary

Ahavat Yeshua	Love of Jesus
Aliyah	Immigration to Israel
Aleph-bet	Alphabet
Anusim	Forced converts
Ashkenazi	Jews from Eastern Europe
Bar/Bat Mitzvah	Son or Daughter of the Commandment, whereby one becomes a full-fledged member of the Jewish community
Beit Immanuel	Emmanuel House
Beit Eliyahu	Elijah House
B'nai Anusim	Descendants of (forced) converts
Chametz	Leaven
Chanukah	Feast of Dedication
Chanukiyah	Nine-branch Chanukah candlestick
Diaspora	Jews living outside of Israel
Haftarah	Old Testament portion, usually from the Prophets
haTikva	*The Hope*, the Jewish national anthem
Kabbalah	The study of ancient Jewish wisdom
Kataluma	Guest room
Kabbalat Shabbat	Receiving or welcoming in the Sabbath
Kehilah	Congregation hall
Ketubah	Marriage contract

Kiddush	Blessing the wine
Kinneret	Harp, the Hebrew name of the Sea of Galilee
L'chaim	To life!
Mashal	Biblical parable or allegory
Mashiach	Messiah
Mazal tov	Good luck
Menorah	Seven-branch candlestick
Mezuzah	A decorative case containing prescribed Hebrew verses
Minim	Probably *ma'aminim*—believers
Mizrad haPanim	Ministry of the Interior
Moshav	Collective farm
Notzrim	Christians
Oleh (m), Olah (f)	Immigrant, plural *Olim*
Olim hadashim	New immigrants
Or haCarmel	Light of Carmel
Rosh haShana	Jewish New Year
Seder	"Order," the Passover celebration ritual
Shabbat	Sabbath
Shavuot	Pentecost
Shekinah	God's Presence, the Glory
Simchat Torah	Joy in the Torah Festival
Shiva	Seven days of housebound mourning for observant Jews
Shofar	Ram's horn trumpet
Sipoor	Story
Sukkot	Tabernacles
Tallit	Prayer shawl
Tanach	The Hebrew Bible, the Old Testament
Torah	The Pentateuch, the first five books of the Bible
Tu B'Shevat	Festival of first fruits and trees

Ulpan	School for the intensive study of Hebrew
Yeshua	Jesus
Yom Kippur	Day of Atonement
Yom Teruah	Feast of Trumpets
Yoridah	Going down, leaving Israel

Bibliography and General Background Reading

The Jewish War by Josephus
Antiquities of the Jews by Josephus
Back to the Land: Called Home to Israel by Katherine Burke Graziano, 2010
Y'Shua, the Jewish Way to Say Jesus by Moishe Rosen, 1982
Jesus Ben Joseph by Walter Riggans, 1993
The Messianic Jewish Movement, an Introduction by Daniel Juster & Peter Hocken, 2004
A Future for Israel? Christian Arabs Share their Stories by Julia Fisher, 2006
The Holy Temple of Jerusalem Chaim Richman, 1997
Israel, A History Martin Gilbert, 2008
ancientchristianitypress.com/earlychristianity.htm
bible-history.com
bibleplaces.com/

Further Reading/Information

Chapter 1
Why Me? by Jacob Damkani, 1997
Persecution of Messianic Jews in Israel:

youtu.be/EII5Km3jN3U

Chapter 2
methodistfriendsofisrael.com
cmj.org.uk
int.icej.org
JewishIsrael.com
The ForeRunners by Reed M. Holmes, 1981
Appointment in Jerusalem by Derek & Lydia Prince, 2006

Chapter 3
christiananswers.net/dictionary/carmel.html
Roman bathhouse in Nazareth:
nazarethbathhouse.org/en/
Jesus house in Nazareth: livescience.com/49997-jesus-house-possibly-found-nazareth.html
Burnt House: en.wikipedia.org/wiki/Burnt_House
Burnt House movie trailer: youtu.be/VrVNK5NYUyg)
bible-history.com/jerusalem/firstcenturyjerusalem_women_s_gate.html
en.wikipedia.org/wiki/Torah_reading
HaAretz Museum: eretzmuseum.org.il/e/

Chapter 4
sixdaywar.org/content/ReunificationJerusalem.asp
templeinstitute.org
grantjeffrey.com/article/article1.htm
come-and-hear.com/sanhedrin/sanhedrin_98.html

Chapter 5
jewishvirtuallibrary.org/jsource/Judaism/messiah.html

Chapter 6
jewishencyclopedia.com/articles/14304-temple-of-herod
bibleresearch.org/observancebook5/b5w79.html
israel-tourguide.info/2011/01/10/earthquakes-history-archaeology/

Chapter 7
God's Tsunami: Understanding Israel and End-Time Revival by Peter Tsukahira, 2009
www.carmel-assembly.org.il
immanuelchurch-jaffa.com
mfa.gov.il/MFA/ForeignPolicy/Terrorism/Victims/Pages/Abigail%20Litle.aspx
Chaim Lanetzach: youtu.be/pZyQXvWnBcQ

Chapter 8
Church of the Annunciation: basilicanazareth.org
families.com/blog/betrothal-and-wedding-customs-at-the-time-of-christ
christiananswers.net/christmas/mythsaboutchristmas.html

Chapter 9
International Fellowship of Christians and Jews: ifcj.org/site/PageNavigator/eng/USENG_homenew

Chapter 10
Hiking the Jesus Trail and Other Biblical Walks in the Galilee by Anna Dintaman and David Landis, 2010
Jesus Boat: youtu.be/66BKA9bWjHI

Chapter 11
Prime Minister Binjamin Netanyahu's May 24 2011 address: youtu.be/0BaMLlnb_KI
Jerusalem Institute of Justice: jij.org

Chapter 12
jewishisrael.ning.com/page/statistics-1
charismanews.com/world/41544-where-your-israel-donation-really-goes
jewishjournal.com/religion/article/messianic_jewish_groups_claim_rapid_growth_20120612
cbn.com/cbnnews/407139.aspx
Israel Always: israelalways.com

Center for Jewish-Christian Understanding:
cjcuc.com/site/
facebook.com/thegalilean/
Messianic Jewish Alliance of America (MJAA):
mjaa.org/site/PageServer
jewsonfirst.org/12a/messianic1.aspx
pewresearch.org
Run with the Horses, Eugene Peterson

Enjoyed this book? Please leave a review on your country's Amazon site and on Goodreads.

About the author

A Messianic Jew, Bobbie Ann Cole speaks and writes widely on meeting Jesus in His everyday world, helping Christians appreciate the rich Jewish symbolism that would have been obvious to His listeners and other believer Jews to understand the challenges they have always faced.

She and husband, Butch, divide their time between her native UK and his native Canada.

Website:
testimonytrain.com/speaker/
or email:
bobbie@testimonytrain.com

Read the Amazon #1 bestseller and Munce prizewinner prequel to *Love Triangles:*

A Gift for You

THE ISRAEL JESUS LOVED
Get closer to Jesus and His homeland with this FREE Ebook

jesus-ebook.com

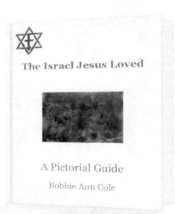

CPSIA information can be obtained
at www.ICGtesting.com
Printed in the USA
FFOW01n0932250915
17179FF